GREYSTONE'S

Creative Hands

EDITOR

Beverley Hilton

GREYSTONE PRESS/NEW YORK · TORONTO · LONDON

Volume 11

Contents

Bobbin Lace
Lace pricking   1174
Collector's Piece
Rear window   1132
Embroidery for a dream   1154
Influence of India   1193
Cats in needlepoint   1200
Crochet: Basic Wardrobe
Hooded hug-me-tight for baby   1124
Girl's lacy sleeved dress   1204
Crochet Know-how
Crib cover in Tunisian stitch   1106
Pillow in chevron crochet   1126
Stole in loopy crochet   1146
Beads and sequins in crochet   1166
Using motifs   1186
Elegant trims   1206
Daisy Work
Designs in Teneriffe lace   1194
Dressmaking
Two more blouse versions   1116
Tucking   1136
The velvet touch   1156
Adaptable patterns for children's clothes   1176
Making hipster pants   1196
Embroidery
Cut work   1108
Italian smocking for a negligée   1128
Shadow appliqué   1148
Butterfly and flower motifs   1168
Spinning wheels of color   1190
Hardanger tablecloth   1208
Fashion Flair
Cherry garland   1120
Hearts and flowers   1160
Home Sewing
Jewelry case   1134
Knitting: Basic Wardrobe
Loopy lounge robes   1104
Two-piece dress   1144
Zippered casual jacket   1164
Lace stitch dress   1184
Knitting Know-how
Looped cap and collar   1102
Shetland knitting   1122
Shetland lace baby shawl   1142
Knitting with beads and sequins   1162
Looped, striped and lacy pillows   1182
Fisherman knitting   1202
Macramé
Working knotted chains   1114
Needlemade Lace
Three Aemilia-Ars lace motifs   1198
Needlepoint
A pride of peacocks   1112
Chevron stitches and doorstop   1172
Patchwork
Patchwork pets   1188
Pattern Library
Palestrina lemons   1101
Cottage flowers   1121
Scarlet spray   1141
Frosted pine   1161
Teneriffe lace mat   1181
Golden rose   1210
Toy Making
Ram   1150

Pattern Library

Palestrina lemons

This very simple design is worked mainly in Palestrina or double knot stitch (see Embroidery 11, p. 208). The leaves are in outline stitch and the lemon seeds of the halved lemon are satin stitch. Matte embroidery thread has been used for this sample but 6-strand floss could be used equally effectively.

Worked on an even-weave linen, still using double knot stitch as an outline, the design can easily be adapted to the use of pulled fabric stitches as interesting fillings.

Looped cap and collar set

Loop stitch knitting produces a bulky fabric useful for making fashion garments, accessories and trims.

Working loop stitch

The loop lies on the right side, or outside, of the fabric but is formed when working a wrong side row. For a sample swatch, cast on 21 sts and K3 rows.

4th row (WS) K1, *insert needle into next st on left-hand needle as if to knit it, wind yarn over needle point and around first and second fingers of left hand twice, then over and around needle point once. Draw all 3 loops through stitch and slip onto the left-hand needle, insert right-hand needle through back of these 3 loops and through the original stitch and knit all together—called ML—K1, rep from * to end of row.

5th row K.

6th row K2, *ML, K1, rep from * to last st, K1.

7th row K.

Rep the last 4 rows four times to see the effect of the design. Bind off.

Variations of loop stitch

Loop stitch can be worked quickly if care is taken not to wind the yarn so tightly around the fingers that it becomes difficult to free the loops when completing the stitch.

Different effects can be obtained by altering the number of stitches between loops and also by changing the number of rows between loop rows. The length of the loops can be varied by working over only two fingers for a short loop or

1102

▲ *Cap and matching collar*

by working over 3 or even 4 fingers for a longer loop. Bulky yarns, or two or more strands of yarn used together, worked over two fingers with loops close together and worked on alternate rows will give a close, deep, bulky pile. A softer effect can be achieved for an evening stole or poncho by using a fine yarn wound around all 4 fingers and worked on every 4th stitch, with 3 plain rows between loops rows.

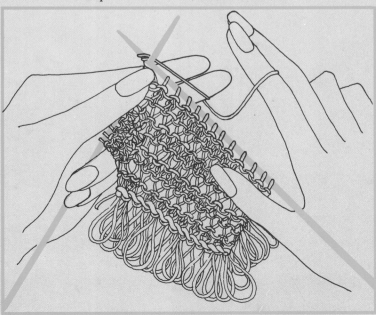

Caps and Collar

Size

Caps. To fit average adult head

Collar. Depth 14in or as desired

> **Gauge**
> 4 sts and 7 rows to 1in over garter st worked with double yarn on No.7 needles.

Materials

Unger Les Coraux
1⅝ oz. balls

Caps. 2 balls for one-color version
1 ball A and 1 ball B for two-color version

Collar. 2 balls A
One pair No.7 needles (or Canadian No.6)
Three buttons for collar
One No.F (4.00 mm) crochet hook

Caps

Using No.7 needles and A, double, cast on 25 sts.

1st row (WS) K1, *insert needle into next st as if to K, wind yarn over needle point and first finger loosely 3 times then over and around needle point once, draw loops through st and return to left-hand needle, insert right-hand needle through back of loops and st and K tog—called ML—K1, rep from * to end.

2nd row K.

3rd row K2, *ML, K1, rep from * to last 3 sts, ytf to avoid making a hole, sl 1. Turn.

4th row Ytf, sl 1, ytb, K to end.

5th row As 1st.

6th row Change to color B if more than 1 color is being used, K.

7th row K20, ytf, sl 1. Turn.

8th row Ytf, sl 1, ytb, K20.

9th row K18, ytf, sl 1. Turn.

10th row Ytf, sl 1, ytb, K18.

11th row K15, ytf, sl 1. Turn.

12th row Ytf, sl 1, ytb, K15.

13th row K12, ytf, sl 1. Turn.

14th row Ytf, sl 1, ytb, K12.

Work 11th, 12th, 9th, 10th, 7th and 8th rows once more.

21st row K all sts.

22nd row Change to color A, K to end.

Rep 1st—22nd rows 4 times more, then 1st—21st rows once.
Bind off.

Finishing

Draw short top edge up and join back seam. Fasten off all ends.

Collar

Using No.7 needles and A double, cast on 15 sts.
Work first 2 rows as given for caps.

3rd row K2, *ML, K1, rep from * to last st, K1.

4th row K.

These 4 rows form patt. Continue in patt until work measures 14in or desired length. Bind off.

Finishing

Using No.F crochet hook and one strand of A, work in sc along one short end, work 2nd row sc, making 3 button loops at regular intervals by working ch3 and skipping 2sc. Fasten off.
Sew on buttons to correspond.

◄ *Winding yarn around two fingers*
One-color version of looped cap ►

Loopy lounge robes long and short

These lounge robes, worked in a jacquard pattern, are trimmed with knitted loops.

Sizes
Directions are for 32in bust. The figures in brackets [] refer to the 34, 36 and 38in sizes respectively.
Long version. Length from top of shoulder 48[49:50:51]in, excluding loop edging.
Short version. Length from top of shoulder 32[33:34:35]in, excluding loop edging. Sleeve seam, 12[13:13:13½]in, excluding loop edging.

Gauge
11½ sts and 12 rows to 2in over patt worked on No.6 needles.

Materials
Reynolds Parfait
30grm balls
Long version. 24[25:27:28] skeins of main color A
12[13:14:15] skeins of contrast B
Short version. 15[17:19:21] skeins of main color A
7[9:10:12] skeins of contrast B
One pair No.3 needles (or Canadian No.10)
One pair No.6 needles (or Canadian No.7)
15 buttons for long version and 11 buttons for short version

Long version

Left front
Using No.3 needles and A, cast on 73[73:79:79] sts.
Work 5 rows garter st.
**Change to No.6 needles. Commence loop patt.
1st row (RS) P.

1104

2nd row K1, *K next st winding yarn 4 times over needle and around 1st, 2nd and 3rd fingers of left hand, then over needle again, draw 5 loops through, then place loops back on left-hand needle and K tog with st tbl—called ML—K1, rep from * to end.
3rd row P.
4th row K.
These 4 rows form loop patt. Rep them twice more, then 1st and 2nd rows once. **
Attach B. Commence patt.
1st row K1A [K1A: K0: K0], *K3B, 1A, rep from * to last 0[0:3:3] sts, K0[K0:K3B: K3B].
2nd row P1A[P1A:P0:P0], *P1A, 1B, 2A, rep from * to last 0[0:3:3] sts, P0[P0:P1A, 1B, 1A:P1A, 1B, 1A].
These 2 rows form patt and are rep throughout.
Continue in patt until work

▼ *Detail of two-color effect*

measures 8in from top of loop edging, ending with a WS row.
Dec one st at beg of next and every following 6th row until 47[50:53:56] sts rem.
Continue without shaping until work measures 40[41: 41½:42]in from top of loop edging, ending with a WS row. ***

Shape front edge
Dec one st at end of next and every other row until 43[46: 49:52] sts rem, ending with a WS row.

Shape armhole and front edge
Next row Bind off 4sts, patt to last 2sts, K2 tog.
Next row Patt to end.
Dec one st at armhole edge on every row; *at the same time* dec one st at front edge on every following 4th row until 28[31:34:35] sts rem.
Continue dec one st at front edge on every following 4th row as before; *at the same time* dec one st at armhole edge on next and every other row until 24[25:27:29] sts rem.
Keeping armhole edge straight, continue dec one st at front edge on every following 3rd row until 18[19:20:21] sts rem.
Continue without shaping until armhole measures 7[7: 7½:8]in from beg, ending with a WS row.

Shape shoulder
Bind off 6[7:6:7] sts at arm edge every other row once, then 6[6:7:7] sts every other row twice.

Right front
Work as given for left front, reversing all shaping.

Back
Using No.3 needles and A, cast on 145[145:155:155] sts.
Work 5 rows garter st.
Work as given for left front from ** to **.
Attach B and work in patt as given for left front until back measures 8in from top of

loop edging, ending with a WS row.
Dec one st at each end of next and every following 6th row until 95[101:107:113] sts rem.
Continue without shaping until back measures same as front to underarm, ending with a WS row. ****

Shape armholes
Bind off 4 sts at beg of next 2 rows.
Dec one st at each end of every row until 71[77:83:85] sts rem, then one st at each end of every other row until 65[69:73:77] sts rem.
Continue without shaping until back measures same as front to shoulder, ending with a WS row.

Shape shoulders
Bind off 6[7:6:7] sts at beg of next 2 rows; 6[6:7:7] sts at beg of next 4 rows.
Bind off rem 29[31:33:35] sts.

Sleeves
Using No.3 needles and A, cast on 93[93:95:95] sts.
Work 5 rows garter st.
Change to No.6 needles and work 6 rows in loop patt as given for left front.
Attach B and continue in patt as given for left front, dec one st at each end of 5th and every following 4th row until 71[73:75:77] sts rem.
Continue without shaping until sleeve measures 12[13:13: 13½]in from top of loop edging, ending with a WS row.

Shape cap
Bind off 4 sts at beg of next 2 rows.
Dec one st at each end of next and every other row until 33 [37:33:31] sts rem, then one st at each end of every row until 23 sts rem. Bind off.

Finishing
Press pieces lightly on WS under a dry cloth with a cool iron, omitting garter st and loop edges. Join shoulder, side and sleeve seams. Sew in sleeves.

Left front edge. Using No.3 needles and A, cast on 10 sts. Work in garter st until edge fits from hem to beg of neck shaping when slightly stretched. Sew in position. Commence loop patt.
***** **1st, 2nd and 3rd rows** K.
4th row (K1, ML) 4 times, K2.
5th and 6th rows K. *****
Rep these 6 rows until edge fits along left front neck to center back neck. Bind off.
Right front edge. Using No.3 needles and A, cast on 10 sts.
Work in loop patt as given for left front edge from ***** to *****, noting that 4th row will read: K2, (ML K1) 4 times.
Mark positions for 15 buttons on left front edge, first to come 14[14½:15:15½]in from lower edge and 15th to come 1in below beg of neck shaping, with 13 evenly spaced between. Continue in loop patt until edge fits up right front, along right front neck to center back neck, making buttonholes when markers are reached as follows:
Buttonhole row (RS facing) K6, bind off 2 sts, K to end. Next row K to end, casting on 2 sts above those bound-off. Bind off.
Using flat st join center back seam of front edges. Sew edges in position. Press seams. Sew on buttons.

Short version

Left front

Using No.3 needles and A, cast on 61[61:67:67] sts. Work 5 rows garter st. Work as given for left front of long version from ** to **.
Attach B and work in patt as given for left front of long version until work measures 8in from top of loop edge, ending with a WS row.
Dec one st at beg of next and every following 6th row until 47[50:53:56] sts rem.
Continue without shaping until front measures 24[25: 25½:26]in from top of loop

▲ *The fanciful loop edging on both versions (short on left, long, right) is made in contrasting color*

edging, ending with a WS row.
Complete as given for left front of long version from ***.

Right front

Work as given for left front, reversing all shaping.

Back

Using No.3 needles and A, cast on 121[121:131:131] sts. Work 5 rows garter st.

Work as given for left front from ** to **.
Attach B and work in patt until back measures 8in from top of loop edging, ending with a WS row.
Dec one st at each end of next and every following 6th row until 95[101:107:113] sts rem.
Continue without shaping until back measures same as front to underarm, ending with a WS row.
Complete as given for back of long version from ****.

Sleeves

Work as given for long version.

Finishing

As given for long version.
Left front edge. Work as given for long version.
Right front edge. Work as given for long version, making 11 buttonholes, the first to come 4[4:4½:4½]in from lower edge and the 11th 1in below beg of neck shaping.

1105

Crib cover using Tunisian crochet

Here is a charming coverlet for a baby's crib, made of pretty crocheted daisy motifs linked together with Tunisian crochet.

Size
Approx 37in by 57in.

Gauge
One daisy measures about 1½in diameter. Be very careful to keep all daisies exactly the same size.

Materials
3-ply baby yarn
12 1oz. skeins
One No.E (3.50 mm) crochet hook
One No.E (3.50 mm) afghan hook

Cover
The center is worked first. Begin by making 3 separate chains of daisies, one of 16 circles for center chain, and 2 of 15 circles for the row at either side, as follows:

1st daisy
Using No.E crochet hook, ch4. Join into a circle with a ss.

1st round (Yrh, insert hook into circle, yrh and draw up a long loop of about ⅜in) twice, yrh and draw through all loops to make 1 petal. Work 15 more petals into circle in same way. Join with ss to 4th of first ch4. Work other daisies in same way. Sew together between 1st and 2nd petals and 9th and 10th petals.

Continue adding daisies in this way until chain is desired length.

Join center daisy chain to side chain of 15 daisies with diamonds of Tunisian crochet.

1st row Using No.E afghan crochet hook, attach yarn to 4th petal at right side of 1st center daisy, draw loop through and keep on hook, insert hook into each of next 3 petals and draw loop through onto hook, insert hook into 1st petal of 2nd daisy beyond join and draw through loop (5 loops on hook).

2nd row *Yrh and draw through first 2 loops, rep from * 3 times, until 1 loop remains on hook.

3rd row *Insert hook through vertical and first horizontal st to left beyond and above vertical st of previous row, yrh and draw through loop, rep from * twice, insert hook into top of next petal on 2nd daisy, yrh and draw loop through.

4th row As 2nd.
These 2 rows form one complete row forward and back.
Rep 3rd and 4th rows twice more.

9th row Insert hook into outside edge of 4th petal of 1st daisy on 15 daisy chain, insert hook into vertical and horizontal thread of 1st st of diamond, yrh and draw through all loops, *insert hook into vertical and horizontal threads of next st, yrh and draw through all loops, rep from * once more, insert hook into next (5th) petal of 2nd daisy on center chain, yrh and draw through loop.
This loop becomes the first

st of the next diamond. Pick up 3 more loops from 2nd central daisy and one from 3rd daisy and work diamond in same way, joining to 2nd of side chain of daisies at beg of 9th row.
Continue along central chain in this way until all daisies are joined and 15 diamonds have been completed, omitting drawing loop through next petal to begin another diamond.
Work semi-circle of petals around end half of last center daisy by working 2 petals into each of next 8 petals. Turn.

2nd semi-circular row
Work 1 petal into each of first 3 petals and 2 petals into each of next 13 petals of previous row (29 petals). Turn.

3rd semi-circular row
Work in Tunisian crochet as follows: Ch4, (insert hook into next ch, yrh and draw loop through) 3 times, (4 loops on hook), insert hook into top of first petal, yrh and draw loop through.
Continue in rows as for diamonds, picking up loop from petal at end of forward rows along side, *work once into next 2 petals, work twice into next petal, rep around semi-circle from *, ending by working once into each of last 2 petals.
Ss down side of semi-circle to next free petal tip on last central daisy, insert hook and draw loop through.
Work in Tunisian crochet in diamonds along other side of central chain, joining on last row of diamonds to center st of daisies on 3rd chain.
Work semi-circular rows at other end to correspond with first end.

At end of Tunisian semi-circle join with ss to daisy.

1st round Ch4, work round of Tunisian crochet, (1 loop on hook), pick up another 3 loops from chain and continue in Tunisian crochet, picking up one loop from center 6 petals along all 15 daisies.
Continue around semi-circle, working twice into every 3rd row, work other side and semi-

circle in same way. Join to 4th of first ch4 with ss.

2nd round Work 1 petal into each st along side and 2 petals into every 4th st around semi-circle, work other side and semi-circle and join with ss to top of 1st petal.

3rd round Ch4, pick up 3 more loops from ch and one from top of first petal, work around in Tunisian crochet picking up one loop from petals on sides and working twice into every 4th petal around semi-circles. Join with ss to 4th of first ch4.

1st half daisy round Ch2, *skip 2 sts, work 7 petals into next st, skip 2 sts, work 1sc into next st, rep from * along side, around semi-circle work in same way, and complete other side and semi-circle in same way. Join with ss to first ch2.

Work diamonds of Tunisian crochet between each half daisy as before, leaving the tip free instead of joining on the last row. Break yarn and fasten off.

Work a chain of daisies as for the center chain, consisting of 64 daisies, and join to form circle. Work 4 separate daisies for corners.

For 1st corner on inner side of daisy circle sew first petal of separate daisy to 6th petal of first daisy in circle. Sew 3rd petal of single daisy to 4th petal of 2nd daisy. Sew 6th petal of single daisy to 4th petal of 3rd and 8th petal to 3rd petal of 4th daisy. Sew 2nd single daisy to 10th, 11th, 12th and 13th daisies of circle. Sew 3rd single daisy to 33rd, 34th, 35th and 36th daisies and 4th single daisy to 42nd, 43rd, 44th and 45th daisies in same way.

Sl st finished circle around already worked center, sewing tips of diamonds to joining sts between daisies and sides of diamonds to petals of daisies.
At corners, sew diamond tip to 4th petal of single daisy, leaving an open diamond at either side. Work all corners in same way until circle is in place.

▲ *Areas of Tunisian crochet link central and outer groups of daisies, giving the cover a pretty drape*

Join yarn to center of outside edge of 3rd daisy of circle and work Tunisian crochet diamonds as before. Work 8 diamonds for end, work 10 times into join between next 2 daisies for corner, work 22 diamonds for side, 10 times between daisies for corner, 8 diamonds for 2nd end, 10 times for corner, 22 diamonds for other side and 10 times between daisies for 4th corner.

2nd row half daisies
Ch4, work 7 petals in same st between diamonds, 1sc in tip of next diamond, 7 petals between diamonds, rep from *, at corners skip 2 sts, 1sc in each of next 3 sts, ch2, 1sc in each of next 3 sts, skip 2 sts. 9 half daisies at each end and 23 half daisies on sides. Join with ss to 4th of first ch4.

Ch4 and into these and edge of daisies as before work 1 round of Tunisian crochet, working 6 times into corner sts. Join with ss to 4th ch. Break yarn.

Continue working in rows leaving one end straight. Attach yarn to corner st at beg of side row with RS facing. Work along side working 1 petal in each st to corner, work 2 petals, ch1, 2 petals in corner st, work 1 petal in each st to 2nd corner, work corner as before and complete side edge to correspond. Turn.

Work 1 row sc along sides and end. Turn with ch4.

Work 1 row Tunisian crochet as previously working 5 times into corner sts. Turn.

Work 1 row sc. Turn.

Rep half daisy row working half daisy into each corner. Break off yarn.

Rejoin yarn at beg of side. Work diamonds of Tunisian crochet between half daisies as before. Break off yarn.

Make a chain of 73 daisies and sl st to Tunisian diamonds, sewing central corner diamond tip to inner side of daisy and sides to rem daisy sts.

Attach yarn to center of outer side of first daisy of new daisy circle and work Tunisian crochet diamonds between daisies along sides and one end as before. Break off yarn.

Attach yarn at beg of side. Work half daisies of 7 petals into center st between diamonds and 1sc into tip of each diamond. Into center corner daisy work 5 petals, ch1, 5 petals, work other corner in same way. Break off yarn.

Rejoin yarn at beg of side. **Next row** Ch4, on these sts and from daisies work 1 row Tunisian crochet working 5 times into corner st. Turn.

Work 1 row sc. Turn.

Work 1 row petals, working 2 petals, ch1, 2 petals in corner sts. Turn.

Work 1 row sc. Turn.

Edging
1st row *In next st work 6 petals, skip 2 sts, 1sc in next st, skip 3 sts, rep from * to end, working 8 petals into each corner. Turn.

2nd row Ch12, *1sc between 3rd and 4th petals of 6 petals of previous row, ch6, rep from * to end working between 4th and 5th sts at corners, work to end. Turn.

3rd row Ch12, *work 6 petals in sc of previous row, 1sc in center of ch, rep from * working 10 petals in corner sts, complete to end. Turn.

4th row As 2nd. Turn.

5th row Ch12, *work 2 petals in sc of previous row above group, ch3, 1ss into 1st of ch3 to form picot, (1 petal, 1 picot) 3 times into same st as first 2 petals, 2 petals into same st, 1sc into ch of previous row, rep from * working corners as follows: skip 2 petals of corner group, into each of next 5 petals work (1 petal, 1 picot) twice, 1 petal into next st, work to end. Do not break yarn but work finishing row along straight edge as follows: 1sc into ch, ch1, insert hook into base of sc, yrh, insert hook into same st, yrh and draw through all loops, rep along edge working twice into ch12 spaces. Fasten off.

1107

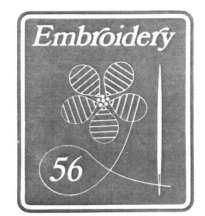

Introduction to cut work

Cut work is more correctly called Richelieu embroidery, named after the famous Cardinal who was Minister to King Louis XIII of France. Cardinal Richelieu, eager to develop industry in France, arranged for skilled Venetian lace-workers to set up schools and workshops encouraging the application of new techniques, thus helping to establish a new skilled industry in France. Cut work remained in vogue throughout the seventeenth century.

There are various forms of embroidery that come under the heading of cut work—Richelieu cut work, Renaissance cut work and reticella cut work. Richelieu is the most solid and reticella the most open. The Richelieu cut work tablecloth shown in this chapter is simple to work from the tracing design on the following pages.

The nature of cut work

Cut work is a form of embroidery where the motifs such as figures, flowers and other shapes are surrounded with closely worked buttonhole stitch linked with bars, the rest of the fabric being cut away.

Stitches used in cut work

Outlines. All the outlines of the motifs in a cut work design are worked in buttonhole stitch.

Bars. Bars are buttonhole stitched or worked in cording and can be decorated with picots (for method of working bars see Embroidery Chapter 48, page 948).

Details. These can be worked in several ways: outline stitch, which can be whipped to give greater relief; backstitch, seeding, satin stitch, French knots or other simple filling stitches.

Threads and fabrics

Coton à broder is used for this form of embroidery or, alternatively, six-strand floss, using two or three strands depending on the thickness of the fabric being stitched.

It is essential to choose fine, stiff, firmly woven fabrics for cut work. Linen is the best but good quality cotton can be used as a substitute.

Preparing the work

Apply the design using a commercial transfer or dressmakers' carbon paper. Baste the fabric onto stiff, strong paper so that it is well stretched with the grain of the fabric straight. With two or three strands of floss in the needle, work small running stitches around the lines of design on the fabric only, until you come to a bar. Fasten the running thread with a tiny backstitch on the right side of the fabric without cutting off the thread, pass over the bar and pick up two or three threads of fabric, pass back to the far side and continue the running stitches (see picture).

Bars are worked at about $\frac{3}{8}$ inch to $\frac{1}{2}$ inch intervals, following the curves of the design. Where a large area of fabric is to be cut away, branched bars are worked to fill in the space.

Working cut work design

When running stitches and foundations for the bars are completed, cover them with closely worked buttonhole stitch, keeping the stitches very neat and even. To give more strength and a raised edge, the buttonhole stitch is worked over a laid thread of one strand of coton a broder or two or three strands of 6-strand floss, in the same way as for cording (see Embroidery Chapter 19, page 366). The buttonhole stitch (see Embroidery Chapter 10, page 190) is also worked with either two or three strands of cotton depending on the thickness of fabric being embroidered. When a bar is reached, pass another thread across the two existing ones and cover all three threads with cording or buttonhole stitch, working over the passing threads only and not picking up the fabric underneath. The buttonhole stitch bars can be decorated with picots. When making the bars, great care should be taken to insure that the tension of the stitches is even—not too loose or too tight—as any unevenness will spoil the work. Fasten off the work by taking a few running stitches along the line of the design where they will be covered by buttonhole stitch. To join onto buttonhole stitch, make a few running stitches and bring the needle up through the back of the work and up through the last buttonhole loop made. Do not fasten off work when making a bar because it looks unsightly.

Branching bars

Work two basting threads between A and B. Work buttonhole stitch from B to C and from there work another two basting threads to E. Work buttonhole stitch from E to D and from there work another two basting threads across to F. Cover the length from F to D, D to C and C to A with buttonhole stitch (see diagram).

Cutting away fabric

When all the embroidery is complete, rip the basting stitches

▼ *Cut work in progress and a bar being worked*

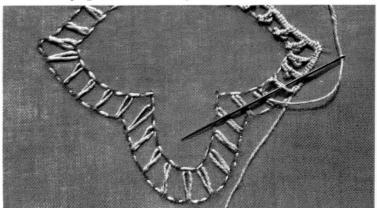

▼ *The motif completed with picots worked on each bar*

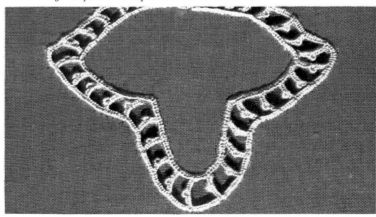

and remove the paper from the back of the work. Press the embroidery carefully on the wrong side of the work over a soft pad, using a damp cloth. Using a small pair of very sharp and pointed scissors, trim the fabric away up to the buttonhole-stitched edges of the design, cutting as close as possible to the stitching so that no rough or raw edges show. When cutting be extremely careful not to damage bars or buttonhole stitches. Work of this kind can be ruined by using blunt scissors or by careless cutting, resulting in a limp piece of work with ragged edges. After cutting is complete, press the embroidery again on the wrong side over a damp cloth.

Uses of cut work

Cut work is mainly used on table linen, but it makes an elegant decoration for sheets and pillow cases. It can also look attractive on clothes—on the collar of a dress, for instance, or on a blouse in the form of panels down sleeves and as an edging for sleeves and hems. For an individual fashion detail, embroider a deep border of cut work on the hem of a wedding dress.

Designs

Designs can be either simple or intricate. The simpler designs generally have sections cut out of the actual motifs, but more complicated designs leave the motif or shapes solid, linked to the background with bars. Most of the designs available in transfers are traditional, very few of them show a modern feeling. Look for inspiration for designs of your own in church windows where the leading of stained glass windows suggests the bars of cut work. The intricate crispness of cut work is accentuated by using white embroidery on white or neutral on neutral fabric. The simplicity and beauty of the work is lost by introducing a variety of colors. Texture can be added by using various line and filling stitches for details.

Cut work tablecloth

To make the tablecloth 52 inches by 72 inches, and six napkins measuring 16 inches square you will need:

- ☐ 3⅛yds 54 inch wide fine linen in white
- ☐ 14 skeins D.M.C. coton à broder or cut work thread shade No. 2644
- ☐ Crewel needle No. 7 or 8
- ☐ Tracing paper
- ☐ Pencil
- ☐ Dressmakers' carbon paper

To transfer the design

Trace the sections of the design from the following pages and transfer the design in the order indicated on the diagram onto the cloth using dressmakers' carbon paper (see Embroidery Chapter 4, p. 68). The rectangular design measures 36 inches by 56 inches.

Working the design

Follow the instructions given in this chapter for preparing and working the design. The outlines and bars are worked in buttonhole stitch, the scrolls in outline stitch and satin stitch, the leaves and spots also in satin stitch. When all the embroidery is completed, press and cut away the shaded areas on the design outline.

To finish the cloth

Finish the edges of the cloth with buttonhole stitch scallops, a plain hem or a hem-stitched hem (see Embroidery 21, p. 414).

Napkins

Cut six pieces of fabric each measuring 18 inches square. Embroider a motif in one corner of each napkin and finish edges in the same method as used for the tablecloth.

▼ *Method of working branching bars*

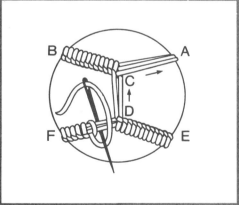

▼ *Detail of a cut work motif*

▼ *This charming tablecloth with matching napkins is easy to embroider*

The outline of the design to trace

The numbers on the sections of the design outlines indicate the placing as shown in the numbered chart. Half of each section is given: trace one half then fold the tracing paper in half and trace the second half.

Top

Top

3

Top

4

Napkin

1111

A pride of peacocks

This charming needlepoint design depicting a pair of strutting peacocks makes an attractive decoration for a chair seat, a pillow, a bag, or, for a more ambitious project, try a headboard worked in chunky yarns on coarse canvas. This chapter contains two more needlepoint stitches useful for backgrounds, both with a woven fabric-like texture.

Stitches to use
This design can be worked in tent stitch, as illustrated, or cross-stitch over one set of double threads on the canvas. For added texture work the background in one of the stitches given in previous Needlepoint chapters such as mosaic or cross-stitch, or either of the fabric-like texture stitches in this chapter. The design can be made larger or smaller depending on the size mesh of the canvas used or by working the stitches over more or fewer threads of the canvas.

Finished size of a design
To determine the finished size of a design worked on a particular mesh of canvas, first count the number of stitches in the design each way. Divide each total by the number of threads to one inch on the canvas you plan to use. For example, the number of stitches in this design is 76 down and 91 across. If the canvas has 10 double threads to 1 inch and you are working one stitch over each set of double threads, this will result in a design measuring approximately 7½ inches by 9 inches.

1112

Drop-in chair seat

To cover a drop-in seat you will need:
- ☐ Muslin
- ☐ Canvas — double-thread canvas with 10 double threads to 1 inch, the area to be worked plus 2 inches on all edges

Note—Worked on double-thread canvas with 10 threads to 1 inch, the peacock design will measure about 7½ inches by 9 inches.

- ☐ D.M.C. Tapestry yarn in the following colors: Peacock blue 7306, dusty pink 7135, yellow 7726 and white
- ☐ Tapestry needle size 18
- ☐ Pins
- ☐ Tacks
- ☐ Tailors' chalk
- ☐ Small hammer
- ☐ About 4yds 1 inch wide tape
- ☐ Adhesive
- ☐ Sewing thread
- ☐ Burlap to cover base of seat

To make the pattern
First take a pattern of the seat top following the instructions given in Needlepoint chapter 21, page 812 and trace the shape onto the canvas.

Mark the center by working a line of basting stitches down the middle of the canvas each way. Mark the center of each side of the chair using tailors' chalk.

Working the design
Cut out a piece of paper measuring 7½ inches by 9 inches and place this on the chair seat, moving it around until you find the best position

for the design. Cut strips of paper to the width of the border motif and place these around the central peacock design until a pleasing balance is achieved. Mark the position of the central motif and the borders onto the canvas with a felt-tipped pen or basting stitches. Work the designs in tent stitch or cross-stitch, working outward from the center, continuing the stitching to the edges of the seat top pattern and then ½ inch beyond.

Block the completed piece of work as described in Needlepoint chapter 5, page 112.

Covering the seat
Lay the seat upside down on the wrong side of the canvas, matching up the center marks on all four sides of the canvas and the seat. Pulling the canvas firmly and evenly over the flat edge of the seat, hammer a tack into the center of each side. Then insert a tack at each of the four

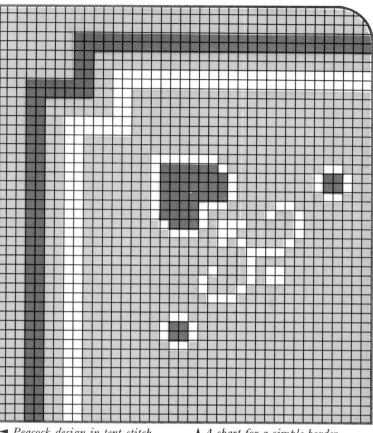

◄ *Peacock design in tent stitch*
▼ *Peacocks for a chair seat*

▲ *A chart for a simple border*
▼ *Tile stitch*

▼ *Web stitch*

corners and work from the corners toward the center tacks, tacking at about ¾ inch intervals. Work opposite sides. Finish the corners following the method given in chapter 21, p. 812. Trim the canvas back to within about 1 inch of stitching and paint with one or two coats of adhesive to prevent the canvas from fraying. Cover the back of the seat with burlap.

Cut a paper pattern for the back of the seat and trace this onto burlap. Turn under a ½ inch hem on all sides and whip the burlap in place.

Tile stitch
This stitch is worked in diagonal rows over single- or double-mesh canvas.

Web stitch
Each row of stitching is worked diagonally over a foundation thread of yarn. This stitch has a much closer texture than tile stitch and can also be worked on single-mesh canvas.

Working knotted chains

Knotted chains can be made with single or double thread. The wall hanging opposite, worked in rug yarn, includes knotted chains.

To make a knotted chain

Chains are made by alternating simple knots from left to right. A left- and right-hand knot make one knotted chain.

Checkered chain pattern

Set on multiples of 12 pairs of threads and fix with one row of horizontal half hitches.
Divide threads into groups of 6 doubled threads and work 6 pairs of single knotted chains in each alternate group. Work a row of horizontal half hitches, followed by a row of single knotted chain on each pair of threads and then a row of horizontal half hitches.
Continue, alternating the knotted groups with the unknotted groups.

Diamond motif pattern

Set on multiples of 12 pairs of threads (each 12 pairs make one diamond). Fix with 2 rows of horizontal half hitches. Work 5 chain knots on the outside pairs of threads, 4 on the next, 3 on the next and 2 on the next pair.
Using the 12th thread as leader, half hitch diagonally to the right over all the threads. With what is now the 12th thread (originally the 13th) as leader, half hitch diagonally to the left over all the threads. Continue to half hitch diagonally to alternate sides until you have reversed all the threads and then repeat the chain knotting on the pairs of threads,

omitting the two innermost pairs.

Chain diamond pattern

Set on multiples of 12 pairs of threads and fix with one row of horizontal half hitch.
Starting from the center of the 12 pairs of threads, make 2 rows of diagonal half hitch outward over the first 4 threads. Make 2 knotted chains over the next pair of threads and 5 diagonal half hitches over the next 4 threads. Knot the 2 outermost pairs of threads with 6 knotted chains. Take the 2 central threads and make a diagonal bar outward over all the threads.
Take the next 2 central threads and work 2 knotted chains. The 2 threads on either side of this knotted chain are then knotted diagonally to left and right, using each of the other threads in turn as leader and remembering to keep the leader above the 2 knotting threads. Then use the pair of threads from the knotted chain in the center as leaders and make a diagonal half hitch to left and right. Next, from the center outward, work 4 pairs of knotted chains, the first (central) pair with 8 knotted chains, the next with 6, the next with 4 and the outermost with 2. The diamonds are linked by twisting the center 2 threads once in the middle at the end of the double row of horizontal half hitches.

Using thick cords and heavy yarns

The main difference in using thicker yarn is that the scale of the work is larger and there is a greater length of material.

A square of asbestos or fiber board propped against a table or the back of a chair makes a good knotting base. A light hammer and tacks are more useful than thumbtacks or dressmaking pins. Draw horizontal and vertical lines as a guide to the horizontal half hitches and the edges so that

the work does not curve. In thick yarn this is much more quickly noticeable.
Wind up the ends of the threads and hold them with a simple buttonhole knot or a rubber band. If the threads reach down as far as the floor use a dustsheet to keep the thread clean.

Macramé 6

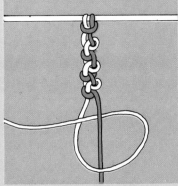

▲ Knotting single thread to left—second stage takes it to the right

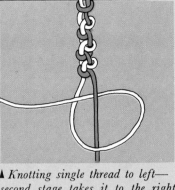

▲ Knotting double threads to right—second stage takes it to the left

▲ Checkered chain pattern

▲ Chain diamond pattern

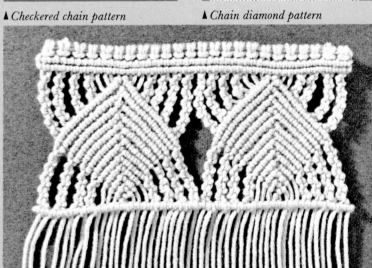

▲ A beautiful example of two diamond motif patterns worked together

Wall hanging

You will need
- [ ] 20 ounces rug yarn
- [ ] 1 18in length brass tubing and 2 curtain rod finials

or

- [ ] 1 24in length bamboo or wooden dowel

Measurements
15in wide by 36in long, including fringe.

To make the hanging
Cut 34 threads 24 feet long, one 34 feet long and one 44 feet long. All the work is done with doubled threads used as one thread to make the knots thicker and the pattern stand out boldly.

There are 8 double lines of horizontal half hitches which are worked by using the first or last doubled thread as leader, taking it across and back. The first doubled thread is longer than all the others as it is used for the vertical half hitches.

Set on tubing 36 doubled threads, making first thread longest and the last thread the second longest. Fix with 2 rows of horizontal half hitches, using the right-hand outside doubled thread as leader and taking it across and back again. Divide threads into groups of 4 doubled threads. Work 10 half square knots on each so that each cord twists, the first and every alternate ones once, every other alternate one twice. Make 2 rows of horizontal half hitches, using first doubled thread as leader. Still using this thread work 2 rows (across and back once) of vertical half hitches (to work vertical half hitches hold the first thread behind the second thread, work 2 half hitches, then hold the first thread behind the third and repeat, etc). Make 2 rows of horizontal half hitches using first doubled thread as leader.

Divide the threads into groups of 4 doubled threads and work 7 rows of alternate square knots. Make 2 rows of horizontal half hitches using first doubled thread as leader. Divide the threads into groups of 6 doubled threads and work a

▲ Here the wall hanging is hung from a brass rod with pointed finials˙

cross in each group in double diagonal half hitches.

Make 2 rows of horizontal half hitches using the first doubled thread as leader. Divide the threads into groups of 3 doubled threads and work 3 square knots on each. Make 2 rows of horizontal half hitches using last doubled thread as leader.

Divide threads into groups of 4 doubled threads. Using the right-hand doubled thread of each group, work 3 half hitches. Divide threads again alternately into groups of 4 and repeat for 4 rows more in this manner. Make 2 rows horizontal half hitches using the last doubled

thread as leader.

Work 2 knotted chains on each pair of doubled threads right across the row, then work 2 rows horizontal half hitches using the last doubled thread as leader.

Cut off the threads at the required length of fringe and unravel the strands.

1115

Two more blouse versions

Here are the two final blouse versions from the Creative Hands Pattern Pack given in Vol. 22—a short sleeved blouse with mandarin collar and a sleeveless blouse that buttons down the back. For a close fitting look the pleats are extended into darts to the hem.

Blouse with mandarin collar

The pattern

Back and Front. You will need the following pattern pieces from the Creative Hands Pattern Pack. from the basic blouse pattern sheet, the Front and Back pattern pieces, numbers 1 and 2; from the accessory sheet, the short version of the straight sleeve and the mandarin collar pattern pieces, numbers 7 and 9.

Facing. Make a front facing pattern and join it to the Front as for the tie-neck blouse (Dressmaking chapter 40, figure 1, p. 796). Also make a back neck facing the same width on the shoulder edge as the front facing as shown in figure 1.

Suitable fabrics

This blouse needs a firm, but not stiff, fabric. Soft woolen fabrics or soft silks are not suitable as the collar would not sit well.
Choose from the following:
- [ ] **Cotton:** soft poplin; shirtings
- [ ] **Linen:** blouse weight linen
- [ ] **Wool:** fine worsted; double knit
- [ ] **Man-mades:** Dacron etc.

Layouts and yardages

Make a layout as shown in Dressmaking 46, p. 916, to work out the minimum yardage requirement. Place the Center Back of the Back, back neck facing and collar pattern pieces on the fold of the fabric. Do not forget to add seam and hem allowances all around.

Notions and other requirements

You will also need:
- [ ] Interfacing for collar and facings
- [ ] Small piece of sheeting
- [ ] 6 small buttons
- [ ] Hook size No. 0
- [ ] Matching thread

Cutting out

Before cutting the collar from the main fabric make a mock collar from sheeting as it may need adjusting. Cut out the collar with seam allowance along the neck seam only, and for extra support cut two layers of the sheeting.

Following your layout cut out the rest of the blouse, not forgetting the hem and seam allowances.
Mark the pattern detail carefully, especially along the neck edge.

Preparing for fitting

Pin and baste the front interfacing to the Center Fronts (Dressmaking Chapter 40, figure 2, page 796), then pin and baste the front facing to the inside of the blouse.
Pin and baste the darts and seams, and also baste the sleeves.
Pin and baste the layers of the mock collar together and use as one. Then pin and baste it to the neckline of the blouse, approximately ¼ inch inside the marked neckline (figure 2). This will become the new stitching line for the stand away mandarin collar.
If you have altered the neckline of the blouse pattern in a previous fitting, this measurement may not be right for you. In this case, baste the collar to the neckline, matching centers and shoulder balance marks first, so there is no fullness on either collar or blouse neckline.
If you have made certain adjustments to the blouse for special back fitting problems, you may also find that the balance marks and the shoulder seams no longer line up.
To correct this move the balance marks forward, making sure that the distance is the same from the shoulder seams on both sides of the neck.

Fitting

Fit the blouse and check the sleeve fitting.
Check the fit of the mandarin collar as follows:
Stand sideways in front of a mirror with your head held up. The collar should mold in a curve around the neckline, remaining upright and with no drag in any place.
The tilt of the collar should be at a good angle to the blouse and not jut out suddenly in any place. It should not touch the neck and should be at an equal distance from it all around.

▼ **1.** *The front and back facings*

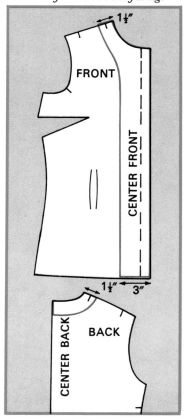

▼ **2.** *Mock collar basted in place*

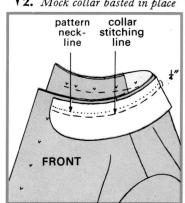

▼ **3.** *Problem A*

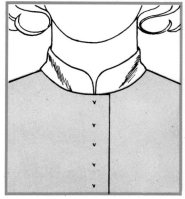

Fitting problems
Problem A. Pulling into the neck at the sides and dragging (figure **3**). The collar needs more length in the upper edge.
Problem B. The collar juts out at the Center Back (figure **4**). The shape of the neckline of the collar must be more rounded toward the Center Back to shorten the length of the upper edge at this point.
Problem C. Small neck and the collar stands away too far (figure **5**). The length of the upper edge of the collar must be decreased and the collar must be cut with more curve.
Problem D. Collar standing away at the sides of the neck (figure **6**). This can happen for two reasons:
i. Narrow front view of neck
ii. Collar too large.
Problem E. Collar is too small (figure **7**). The collar needs to be made larger.

Correcting the faults
When fitting for problems B, C and D pinch and pin the fullness into small pleats till the collar stands nicely out of the neckline of the blouse.
All five problems will then require the making of a new pattern.

Making a new collar pattern
Problem A. Pin the Center Back of the pattern to the straight edge of a sheet of paper and snip the pattern from the upper edge toward the balance mark on the lower edge (figure **8**). Spread the cut until the lower edge is almost straight and curves only a little at the Center Front. Pin the pattern down securely and draw around the new shape.
Problem B. Make a small tapering pleat copied from the mock collar on the upper edge of the collar pattern between Center Back and shoulder seam balance mark, and pin the Center Back of the pattern to the straight edge of a sheet of paper (figure **9**).

Draw around the new shape rounding the curve where it dips into the pleat on the pattern as shown.
Problem C. Copy the small pinned and tapering pleats on the mock collar onto the pattern and pin the Center Back to the straight edge of a sheet of paper (figure **10**).
Draw around the new shape, curving the lines gently where they dip into the pleats as shown.
Problem D. i. Copy the small pinned and tapering pleats on the mock collar onto the pattern and pin the Center Back of the pattern to the straight edge of a sheet of paper (figure **11**).
Draw around the new shape, curving the lines gently where they dip into the pleats as shown.
ii. Make a pleat in the collar pattern the same depth on both edges and then make a new pattern as above (figure **12**).
Problem E. Cut the pattern to enable you to spread and lengthen it to the required amount. Pin the Center Back of the pattern to the straight edge of a sheet of paper. Spread it and draw around the new shape as shown (figure **13**).

A closer fit
Finally, if you want the mandarin collar to fit closely to the neck, fold off the extra length in the original pattern, making small pleats between Center Back and balance mark and balance mark and Center Front, until the neck edge of the collar equals the size of the original neck edge on the blouse, and make a new pattern. Use the new pattern to cut the collar for your blouse.

Making the blouse
Working in the Center Fronts first, sew the interfacing in position with small prick stitches as shown in Dresmaking Chapter 40, page 796.
Stitch, press and finish the side seams and shoulder seams.
Stitch the back neck facing to the front facing at the shoulder seams. Trim the seam allowances and press the seams open.

▼**4.** *Problem B*
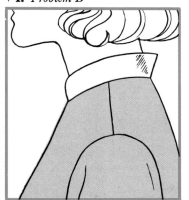

▼**6.** *Problem D*
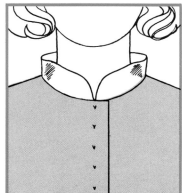

▼**5.** *Problem C*
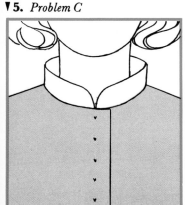

▼**7.** *Problem E*
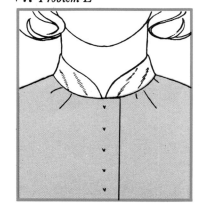

▼**8.** *Correcting problem A*
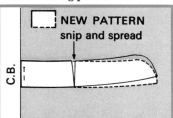

▼**9.** *Correcting problem B*
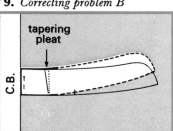

▼**10.** *Correcting problem C*
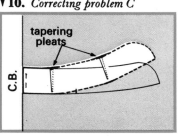

▼**11.** *Correcting problem D.i*
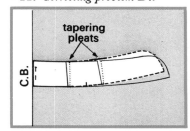

▼**12.** *Correcting Problem D.ii*
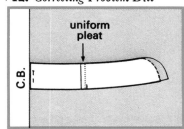

▼**13.** *Correcting problem E*
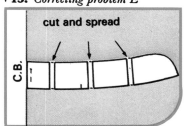

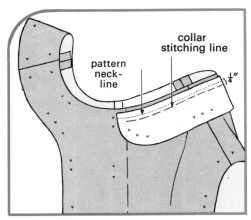

▲ **14.** *Basting the interfaced collar in place*

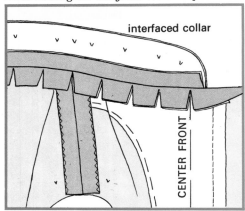

▲ **15.** *The neck seam snipped and pressed open*

Attaching the collar

In the following text read "collar" for the outer section and "collar facing" for the inner section of the collar.

To check that all balance and center marks are lined up on the neck facing and the blouse, pin the facing to the neck edge. Unpin the facing and work on each layer as follows.

Pin and baste the interfacing to the inside of the collar.

The neckline of the blouse and facing for the mandarin collar falls $\frac{1}{4}$ inch inside the original pattern neckline.

Pin and baste the interfaced collar to the blouse neck edge with right sides together and all balance marks matching (figure **14**). Baste and then stitch.

Starting at the Center Front, snip the full length of the seam allowance on the blouse neckline (figure **15**). Press the seam open.

Pin and baste the collar facing to the neckline of the blouse facing, working just inside the seamline on the collar facing and allowing the Center Front edge of the collar facing to go a fraction over the Center Front on the blouse facing (figure **16**). This will make the collar facing fit slightly tighter when finished and allow the collar to roll over it to hide all seam edges.

Stitch the collar facing to the facing.

Snip the seam allowance on the neckline of the facing as you did on the blouse neckline and press the seam open.

Pin the collar to the collar facing, with right sides facing, using the seamlines as marked on the upper edge of both. But allow the seamline on the Center Front edge of the collar facing to fall outside the seamline of the collar by meeting the Center Front markings on the neckline of the blouse and the neck facing.

Baste the collar and collar facing together carefully along the collar stitching line. Then stitch, working with the facing uppermost but stitching along the basted line; stitch from the end of the wrap on one side to the Center Front, pivot the work on the needle, and work along the basted seamline of the mandarin collar, pivoting the work as you reach the Center Front on the opposite side.

Continue working along the wrap toward the end (figure **17**).

Trim the seam allowances and layer them as for the interfaced edges of the shirt dress in Dressmaking chapter 42.

After layering, make small notches into the seam allowance on the curved edges of the collar and turn the collar to the right side, thus turning the facings to the inside of the blouse.

The seamline along the collar edge will

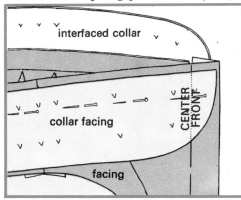

▼ **16.** *The collar facing pinned to the facing*

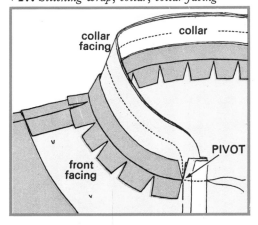

▼ **17.** *Stitching wrap, collar, collar facing*

already be rolling toward the collar facing. The fullness in the collar will make it roll smoothly around the neck edge.

Edge-baste along the seamline, making sure that it is not pushed to the edge of the collar.

Baste the facing in position along the front edges and press lightly.

Finishing

To prevent the seam allowances along the neckline of the blouse and the facing from wrinkling up during wash and wear, it is necessary to secure them.

To do this, meet both seamlines along the neck edge and pin them together carefully. Place the shoulder seam of the blouse to the shoulder seam of the facing and Center back to Center Back to insure that the collar does not wring.

Baste the seamlines together on the outside of the facing.

Then, working under the facing on the seam allowances, sew the seam allowances together by hand, using small running stitches. Leave the stitches a little loose, and make a small backstitch now and again to stop the seamline from moving. Hand sew the facing edge to the shoulder seams.

Stitch the sleeve seams.

Pin, baste and stitch the sleeves into the blouse. Finish and press the seams.

Finish the blouse hemline as shown for the basic blouse in Dressmaking chapter 19, page 368.

Mark out the buttonholes, starting 1 inch from the Center Front neck edge. Make the buttonholes and sew on buttons to correspond.

To keep the corner of the wrap in place when the blouse is buttoned, hand-work a bar and sew a small hook to the underside of the top corner.

Blouse with Back fastening

You will need the Front and Back patterns for the basic blouse, pattern pieces 1 and 2 in the Pattern Pack.

The New Front pattern

The New Front is cut on a fold, so copy the original Front pattern up to the Center Front only (figure **18**) to exclude the wrap.

The New Back pattern

Copy the Back pattern, extending it for 1 inch along the Center Back (figure **19**) to make a wrap for the Center Back opening.

The Front and Back facings

If you are not going to make a rouleau type bound neck edge, copy the New Front

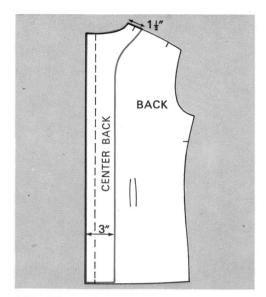

▲ *The sleeveless blouse with back buttoning*

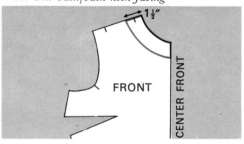

▲ **20.** *The back/back neck facing*

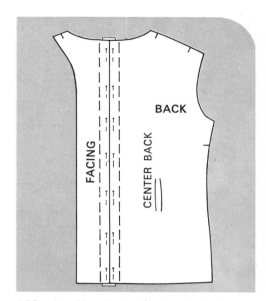

▲ **22.** *Attaching the back/back neck facing*

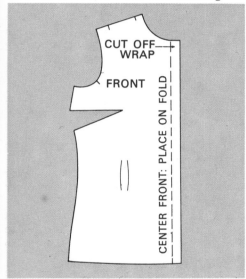

▲ **18.** *The Front pattern for cutting on fold*
▼ **19.** *The Back pattern for back buttoning*

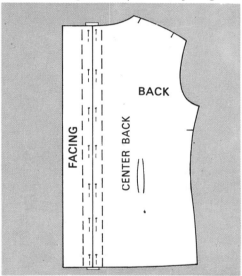

▲ **21.** *The front neck facing*

and New Back pattern pieces where necessary to make the front neck and back facings as shown (figures **20** and **21**). Attach the back facing to the Back (figure **22**).

If you are binding the neck edge with a rouleau type finish you will not need neck facings, so make a back facing as in figure **20** but excluding the neck section. Then attach it to the Back as shown (figure **23**).

The pattern outline is now complete.

Buttons and buttonholes

More ease is needed across the Back for back buttoning or else too much strain will be placed on the buttons and they will pop off.

To add this ease mark the positions of the buttons and buttonholes $\frac{1}{4}$ inch outside the Center Back line. No extra ease is needed at the neck edge, so this button position needs to be $\frac{1}{4}$ inch inside the Center Back line at the neck edge to compensate for the buttonhole which has been moved over, and then the other buttons are positioned as shown (figure **24**).

Making the blouse

Once you've converted the pattern simply follow the usual sewing procedure.

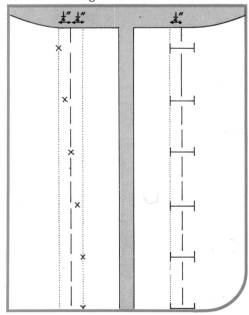

▲ **23.** *Attaching a back facing only to the Back*
▼ **24.** *Positioning the buttons and buttonholes*

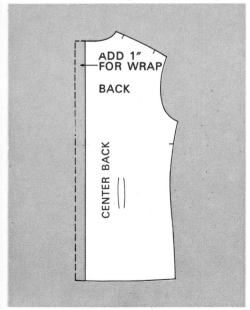

Furnishing Fashion Flair

Cherry garland

Crisp bunches of cherries worked in bright colors look good in long and short stitch or satin stitch. Simply trace and transfer the life size design outline from this page. For appliqué work, enlarge the design slightly so that the shapes are a manageable size.

1. *A round tablecloth decorated with a scalloped border and a central circle of cherries.*

2. *A napkin case with the flap edge embroidered to match the tablecloth.*

3. *The napkin case unfolded, showing individual pockets embroidered with initials to hold each napkin.*

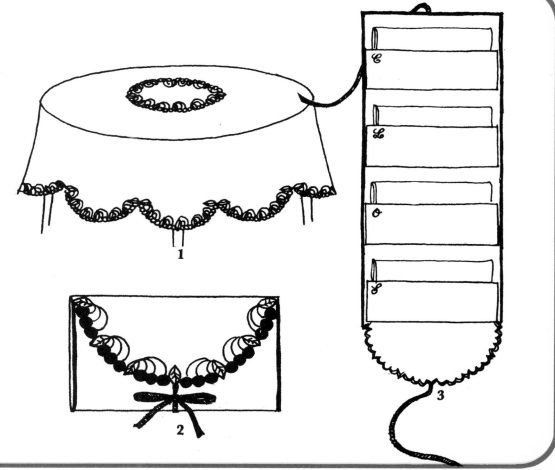

Pattern Library

Cottage flowers

Textured fabrics make an interesting basis for embroidery and here a spray of flowers has been worked on a background fabric of waffle weave cotton. The design is stitched in D.M.C. 6-strand floss using three strands throughout in gold 422, pale gold 738, green 502, pale green 503, lilac 3041, pale lilac 211, light blue 928, pale blue 927, blue 926, dark blue 924, pink 3688 and pale pink 3689. The embroidery is mainly in satin stitch with some of the larger leaves worked in long and short stitch with the veins embroidered in outline stitch.

Introduction to Shetland knitting

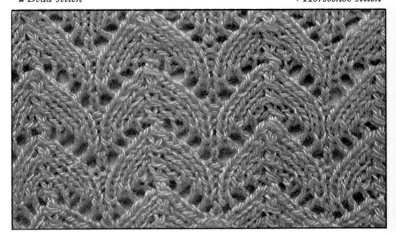

▲ *Bead stitch*   ▼ *Horseshoe stitch*

The most gossamer and the finest examples of lace knitting come from Unst, the most northerly of all the Shetland islands. In the early nineteenth century a visitor to the island brought with her a collection of fine Spanish lace. This delicate surface inspired the islanders to create knitted lace of similar beauty using their single ply homespun yarn. Although such very fine yarns are rarely used today, Shetland lace stitches can be used to make a variety of lovely garments in an average weight yarn.

Although Shetland lace stitches are adaptable, they are seen at their best if worked with reasonably fine yarns and needles. No.3 needles and fingering yarn are recommended for the stitches in this chapter to produce a fine, knitted lace.

Casting on for lace should be kept as loose as possible. Ideally use a simplified two-needle method. Cast on 2 stitches, insert the right-hand needle into the second stitch instead of between the stitches, draw one stitch through and transfer it to the left-hand needle. Wherever possible, weave edges together and bind off loosely so that the edges are soft and smooth.

Bead stitch

This is a simple lace to use for filling diamonds or hexagonal areas, or for working large areas such as shawl centers. The illustration uses it as an all-over pattern. It can easily be adapted to have a less open appearance by working 2, 3 or more knitted stitches between the panels.

It is worked over a number of stitches divisible by 7 (for example, 28).

1st row. (RS) *K1, K2 tog, ytf, K1, ytf, sl 1 knitwise, K1, psso, K1, rep from * to end.
2nd row. *P2 tog tbl, yrn, P3, yrn, P2 tog, rep from * to end.
3rd row. *K1, ytf, sl 1 knitwise, K1, psso, K1, K2 tog, ytf, K1, rep from * to end.
4th row. *P2, yrn, P3 tog, yrn, P2, rep from * to end.
These 4 rows form the pattern and are repeated as desired.

Crest of the wave stitch

Old shale stitch, reminiscent of the print left on sand by receding waves, is a simple design (see Knitting Know-how chapter 13, page 242) which is also the basis for many equally simple but less often seen versions. Of these, crest of the wave stitch is perhaps the most effective.

It is worked over a number of stitches divisible by 12, plus 1 (for example, 37).

1st, 2nd, 3rd and 4th rows. K.
5th row. K1, *(K2 tog) twice, (ytf, K1) 3 times, ytf, (sl 1 knitwise, K1, psso) twice, K1, rep from * to end.
6th row. P.
Rep 5th and 6th rows 3 times more.

These 12 rows form the pattern and are repeated as desired.

Razor shell stitch

Another stitch which takes its name from a well known beach shell, this can be varied over 4, 6, 8, 10 or 12 stitches. Instructions are given for both 6 and 10 stitch variations.

The six stitch version is worked over a number of stitches divisible by 6, plus 1 (for example, 25).
1st row. (WS) P.
2nd row. K1, *ytf, K1, sl 1, K2 tog, psso, K1, ytf, K1, rep from * to end.
Repeat 1st and 2nd rows as desired.
The ten stitch version is worked over a number of stitches divisible by 10, plus 1 (for example, 31).
1st row. (WS) P.
2nd row. K1, *ytf, K3, sl 1, K2 tog, psso, K3, ytf, K1, rep from * to end.
These 2 rows form the pattern and are repeated as desired.

Horseshoe stitch

The imprint of horseshoes on damp sand is a familiar sight to the islanders and is used in this stitch to create a lace which has innumerable uses.

It is worked over a number of stitches divisible by 10, plus 1 (for example, 31).
1st row. (WS) P.
2nd row. K1, *ytf, K3, sl 1, K2 tog, psso, K3, ytf, K1, rep from * to end.
3rd row. As 1st.
4th row. P1, *K1, ytf, K2, sl 1, K2 tog, psso, K2, ytf, K1, P1, rep from * to end.

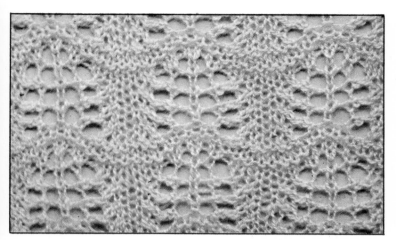

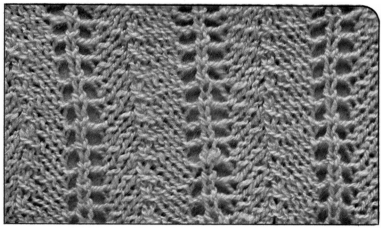

▲ *Crest of the wave stitch*   ▼ *Faggoting cable stitch*   ▲ *Razor shell stitch*   ▼ *Fern stitch*

5th row. K1, *P9, K1, rep from * to end.

6th row. P1, *K2, ytf, K1, sl 1, K2 tog, psso, K1, ytf, K2, P1, rep from * to end.

7th row. As 5th.

8th row. P1, *K3, ytf, sl 1, K2 tog, psso, ytf, K3, P1, rep from * to end of the row.

These 8 rows form the pattern and are repeated as desired.

Faggoting cable stitch

Mainly a lace stitch, this gives an additional interest and texture to the lace by the introduction of the cable. The cable can be worked crossing in front or behind the work or can be alternated to incorporate both. It is often used as a single panel at either side of another motif or can form an all-over pattern as illustrated. It is worked over a number of stitches divisible by 6, plus 8 (for example, 32).

1st row. (WS) P2, *K2, ytf, K2 tog, P2, rep from * to end.

2nd row. K2, *P2, yrn, P2 tog, K2, rep from * to end.

3rd and 4th rows. As 1st and 2nd.

5th and 6th rows. As 1st and 2nd.

7th row. P2, K2, ytf, K2 tog, P2, *sl next 2 sts onto cable needle and hold at front of work, K2, K2 from cable needle—called C4F—P2, K2, ytf, K2 tog, P2, rep from * to end.

8th row. As 2nd.

9th and 10th rows. As 1st and 2nd.

11th and 12th rows. As 1st and 2nd.

13th and 14th rows. As 1st and 2nd.

15th row. P2, C4F, P2, *K2, ytf, K2 tog, P2, C4F, P2, rep from * to end.

16th row. As 1st.

These 16 rows form the pattern and are repeated as desired.

Fern stitch

Often used as a shawl border, the shape of the motif allows for easy corner shaping. The size of the motif can vary from a miniature fern to a very large shape but the method of working remains the same, extra stitches being worked in. This is worked over a number of stitches divisible by 15 (for example, 45).

1st row. (RS) *K7, ytf, sl 1 knitwise, K1, psso, K6, rep from * to end.

2nd row. P.

3rd row. *K5, K2 tog, ytf, K1, ytf, sl 1 knitwise, K1, psso, K5.

4th row. P.

5th row. *K4, K2 tog, ytf, K3, ytf, sl 1 knitwise, K1, psso, K4, rep from * to end.

6th row. P.

7th row. *K4, ytf, sl 1 knitwise, K1, psso, ytf, sl 1, K2 tog, psso, ytf, K2 tog, ytf, K4, rep from * to end.

8th row. P.

9th row. *K2, K2 tog, ytf, K1, ytf, sl 1 knitwise, K1, psso, K1, K2 tog, ytf, K1, ytf, sl 1 knitwise, K1, psso, K2, rep from * to end.

10th row. P.

11th row. *K2, (ytf, sl 1 knitwise, K1, psso) twice, K3, (K2 tog, ytf) twice, K2, rep from * to end.

12th row. *P3, (yrn, P2 tog) twice, P1, (P2 tog tbl, yrn) twice, P3, rep from * to end.

13th row. *K4, ytf, sl 1 knitwise, K1, psso, ytf, sl 1, K2 tog, psso, ytf, K2 tog, ytf, K4, rep from * to end.

14th row. *P5, yrn, P2 tog, P1, P2 tog tbl, yrn, P5, rep from * to end.

15th row. *K6, ytf, sl 1, K2 tog, psso, ytf, K6, rep from * to end.

16th row. P. These 16 rows form patt and are repeated as desired.

Hooded hug-me-tight for baby

Crocheted in a crisp cluster stitch to make a firm yet lightweight surface, this hooded jacket is a perfect garment to keep baby warm and snug. It is designed to be suitable for a boy or a girl. The body of the jacket is made in one piece and then divided at the armhole. The hood is crocheted separately, and is attached to the completed jacket.

Sizes

Directions are for 20in chest. The figures in brackets [] refer to the 22in size only. Length, 10¾[11½]in.

Sleeve seam, 6½[7½]in.

Gauge
6 motifs and 12 rows to 4in over patt worked on No.F crochet hook
Note
One motif consists of 2 clusters worked into the same stitch.

Materials

3-ply baby yarn
4 ounces
One No.E (3.50 mm) crochet hook
One No.F (4.00 mm) crochet hook
Three buttons

▼ *Detail showing rows of cluster stitch alternating with single crochet*

Body

Using No.F crochet hook, ch85[99].
1st row Yrh, insert hook into 5th ch from hook, yrh, pull loop through, (yrh, insert hook into same ch, yrh, pull loop through) twice, yrh and pull through all 7 loops on hook to form 1 cluster—called 1cl—ch2, 1cl into same st as last 1cl, ch1, *skip ch2, 1cl into next ch, ch2, 1cl into same ch as last 1cl, ch1, rep from * ending with 1dc into last ch. Turn. 28[32] motifs.
2nd row Ch1, *2sc into next ch2 sp, 1sc into next ch1 sp, rep from * to end. Turn.
3rd row Ch3, 1cl into 2nd sc, ch2, 1cl into same sc, ch1, *skip 2sc, 1cl into next sc, ch2, 1cl into same sc, ch1, rep from * ending with 1dc into last st. Turn.
4th row As 2nd.
Rows 3 and 4 form patt and are rep throughout.
Continue in patt until work measures 6[6½]in from beg.

Divide for armholes

1st row Work in patt over first 7[8] motifs only, 1dc into next st. Turn.
Complete right front on these sts.
Continue until work measures 8¾[9½]in from beg, ending at armhole edge.

Shape neck

Continue in patt working one motif less at neck edge every other row twice.
Fasten off.

Left front

Attach yarn to sts for left front, working 1dc into first st, then working in patt over last 7[8] motifs only.
Complete to correspond with right front.

Back

Attach yarn to center 14[16] motifs and work in patt until back measures same as fronts to shoulder. Fasten off.

Sleeves

Using No.F crochet hook, ch25[28].
Work in patt as given for body. 9[10] motifs.
Work 4 rows.
Continue in patt, inc 1cl at each end of next and every following 4th row until 2cl at each side have been inc.
Continue without shaping until sleeve measures 6½[7½]in, or desired length to top of sleeve. Fasten off.

Hood

Using No.F crochet hook, ch49[55].
Work in patt as given for body. 17[19] motifs.
Work 2 rows.
Keeping patt correct, inc 1cl at each end of every other row until there are 21[23] motifs.
Continue without shaping until hood measures 5¼[5½]in from beg.

Shape back

1st row Ss over first 7[8] motifs and continue on center 7 motifs only.
Dec 1cl at each end every other row 3 times.
Continue without shaping until hood measures 10[10¾] in from beg. Fasten off.

Finishing

Join shoulder and sleeve seams. Sew in sleeves.
Cuffs Using No.E crochet hook, work 3 rows sc along lower edge of sleeves.
Last row Without turning work, work 1 row of crab st by working from left to right, working 1sc into each sc to end. Fasten off.
Body Work as given for cuffs from center front neck edge around body to other neck edge, making 3 evenly spaced buttonholes on 3rd row, on right front for a girl and left front for a boy, by working ch4 and skipping 4sts.
Hood Work around front edge of hood as given for cuffs. Seam back of hood to side edges. Sew hood around neck edge of body. Sew on buttons.

Blue for a boy in bulky crochet ▶

Razzamatazz pillow in chevron crochet

Multi-color scheme from odds and ends of yarn for a gay effect ► A modern look with four colors and a pompon trim▼

Here is a fresh and charming furnishing idea for using up odd pieces of yarn. This exotic pillow also provides you with an opportunity to practice increasing and decreasing in simple single crochet to shape fabric in an exciting way.

Size
Approximately 14½in across the width of the pillow.

Gauge
5 ridged sc and 3 rows to 1in over patt worked on No.F crochet hook.

Materials
Bucilla Soufflé
Two balls each of main color A, and contrast colors B, C and D
One No.F (4.00 mm) crochet hook
One round pillow form 14in wide or foam filling and lining to make a pillow insert to these measurements.

Pillow

Using No.F crochet hook and A, ch214.
Base row Into 2nd ch from hook work 1sc, 1sc into each of next 9ch, *into next ch work 3sc, 1sc into each of next 10ch, insert hook into next ch and draw yarn through, skip 1ch, insert hook into next ch and draw yarn through, yrh and draw through all loops on hook, 1sc into each of next 10ch, rep from * to last 11ch, work 3sc into next ch, 1sc into

each of next 10ch. Turn.

1st patt row Ch1, dec one st
by inserting hook into back
loop only of next sc and
drawing yarn through, insert
hook into back loop only of
next sc and draw yarn
through, yrh and draw
through all loops on hook,
work 1sc into each of next
9sc working into back loop
only of each sc, *3sc into
next sc (which is the center
sc of the inc sc in previous
row), working into back loop
only, 1sc into each of next
10sc working into back loop
only, dec in next 3sc by
inserting hook into back loop
only of next sc and drawing
yarn through, skip 1sc, insert
hook into back loop only of
next sc and draw yarn
through, yrh and draw
through all loops on hook,
1sc into each of next 10sc
working into back loop only,
rep from * to end of row, dec
one st in last 2sc by inserting
hook into back loop only of
last sc but one and drawing
yarn through, insert hook into
back loop only of next sc and
draw yarn through,
yrh and draw through all
loops on hook. Turn.
This row forms patt and is
rep throughout.
Keeping patt correct work 6
rows in all in A, 6 rows in B,
2 rows in C, then 4 rows each
in D, A, C, B, D, A and C.
Fasten off leaving an end
long enough to join seam.
Darn in all ends.

Finishing

DO NOT PRESS.
Join side seams to form a
circle being careful to match
stripes.
Join the sides of each chevron
point at one end tog and
catch the point of each
chevron and fasten off securely.
Insert pillow form and
complete chevron points at
other end in same way.
Trim one side of the pillow
with a large crochet covered
button (see Crochet Know-
how chapter 28, page 546)
in A and the other side with
a pompon using A, B, C
and D.

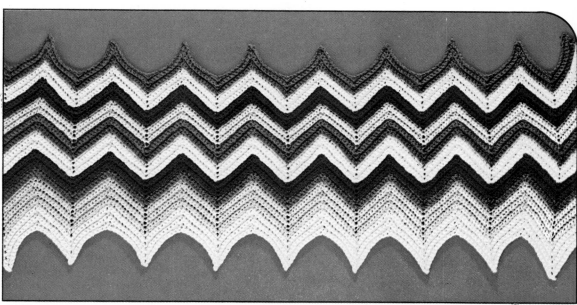

▲ *When the crochet is completed it makes a strip. The sides of each point are seamed and the strip joined to form a circle. The points are gathered at top and bottom to meet.*
▼ *Pillow with button trim*

Italian smocking for a negligee

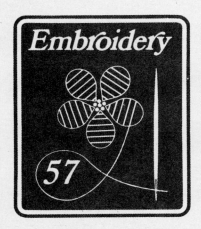

Embroidery 57

This pretty method of decorating gathers is really smocking in reverse. Rows of firm smocking stitches are worked on the back of the fabric to control the gathers, then the embroidery is worked on the right side over the surface of the tiny pleats, giving a firm control to the fabric. A graph pattern and full instructions for making the negligee illustrated are given in this chapter. The same pattern can be used for ordinary smocking if desired.

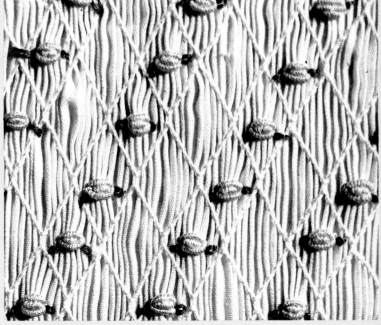

▲ *Another pretty example of Italian smocking*
▼ *Detailed illustration of the embroidery design*

▼ *The tracing outline for the embroidery design*

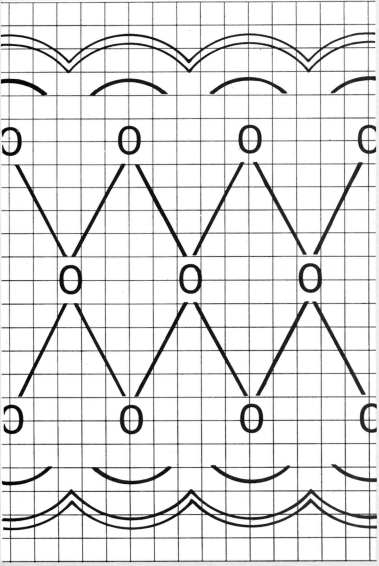

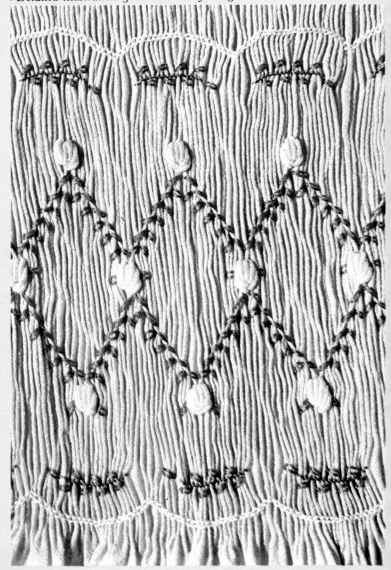

Working the smocking

Work the foundation of smocking on the wrong side, exactly over the dots so that they are covered with stitches and do not show through to the right side of the sheer fabric. Using pink pearl cotton, pick up the transfer dots using cable stitch. This is important as the embroidery on the right side will not keep the pleats firm without this backing work. Work across each row of dots until the whole panel is covered. When all the foundation smocking is completed pull out the gathering threads. Referring to the diagram, copy the design onto the right side of the work with basting thread. Embroider the design as shown in the illustration using chain stitch for the leaves, outline stitch for the stems, bullion knots for the roses and two lines of outline stitch for the scalloped edge.

Full length view, showing the simple ribbon bow neck fastening ►
▼ *Back view of negligee showing the effect of the smocked panel*

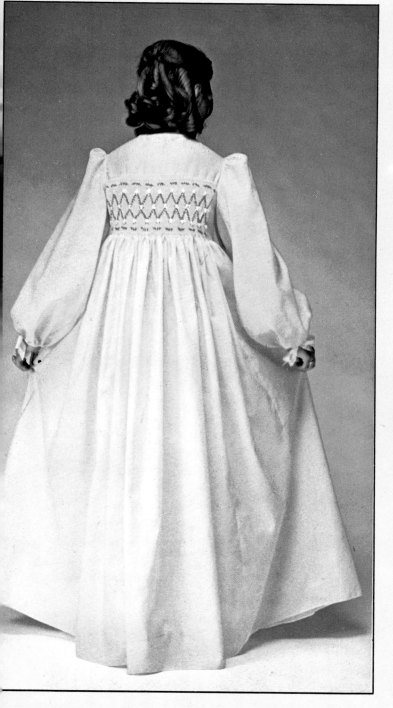

▼ *A negligee to daydream in*

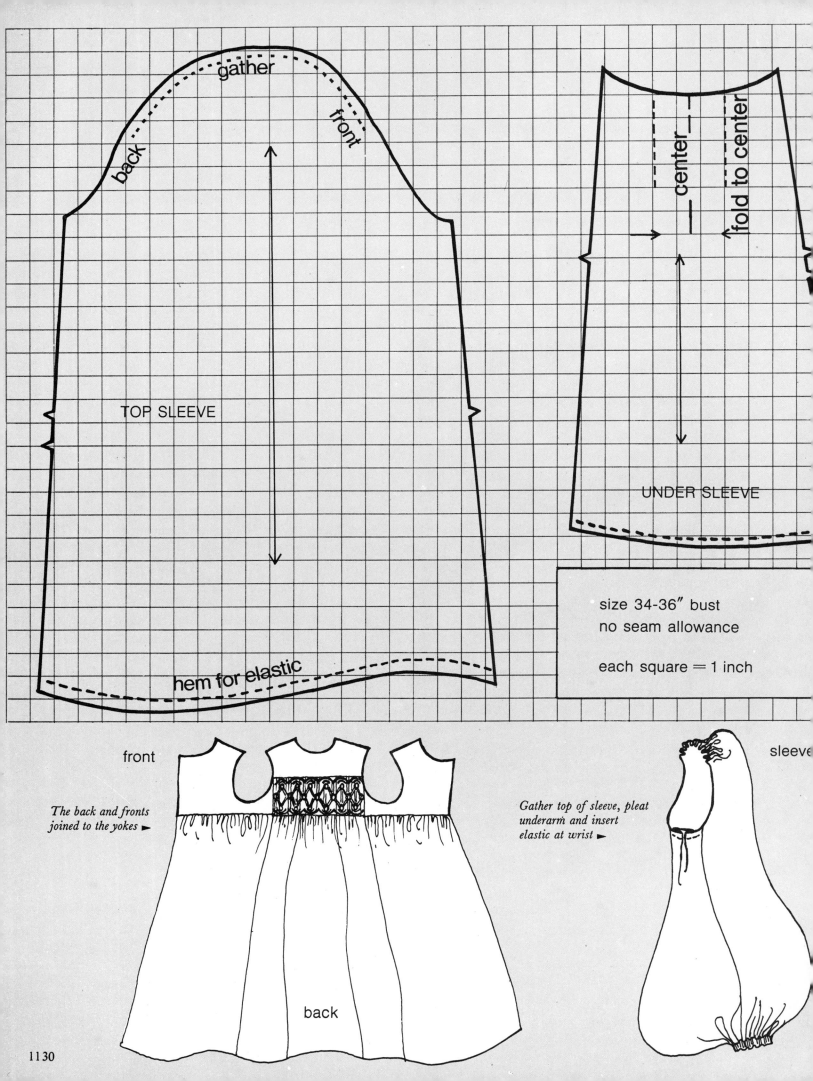

gather

back

front

TOP SLEEVE

hem for elastic

center

fold to center

UNDER SLEEVE

size 34-36" bust
no seam allowance

each square = 1 inch

front

*The back and fronts
joined to the yokes* ▶

back

sleeve

*Gather top of sleeve, pleat
underarm and insert
elastic at wrist* ▶

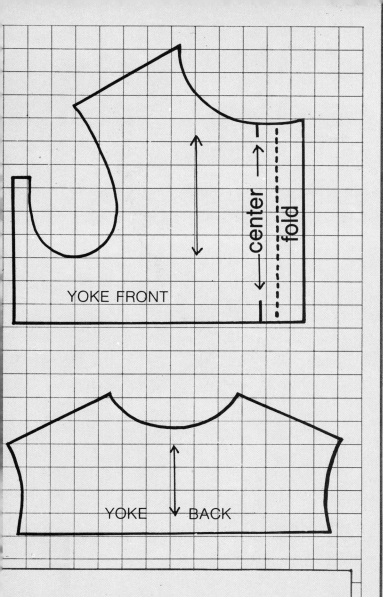

YOKE FRONT

center fold

YOKE BACK

Skirt

front: cut 2 lengths 36"x46" each

back: cut 1 length 36"x 52"

cut 2 lengths 18"x 52" each

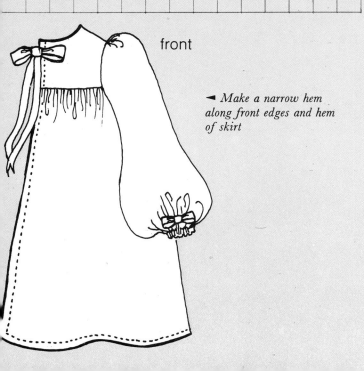

front

◄ *Make a narrow hem along front edges and hem of skirt*

To make this negligee to fit a 34 to 36 inch bust you will need:

☐ 7¾yd 36 inch wide lawn, pink
☐ 3½yd double satin ribbon, white for bows
☐ Strip of transfer dots ¼ inch apart, 72 inches long by 6½ inches deep
☐ 3 snap fasteners
☐ D.M.C. Pearl cotton—1 skein each of white, green and pink
☐ Sewing thread for making garment and for gathering
☐ ½yd narrow elastic
☐ 1 inch squared paper
☐ Pencil

Size

For a smaller size, cut the pattern without a seam allowance and with about 6 inches less on the width of the area to be smocked. For a larger size, cut the seam allowance ¼ inch larger and allow about 6 inches extra on the width of the area to be smocked.

To make the pattern

Copy the pattern from the graph onto 1 inch squared paper. Cut out the pattern and lay it on the fabric according to the layout guide. Cut out allowing ⅝ inch seam allowance on all edges.

Negligee back

Seam by machine stitching the two narrow back panels to each side of the wider back panel. Work a second line of stitching ¼ inch out from the first line. Trim the fabric to this second line of stitching and finish the seam edges by zigzag machine or overcast by hand. Iron the transfer across the top of the panels onto the wrong side of the work. Pick up the smocking dots as instructed in Embroidery 22, p. 428, but for this garment pick up just above the transfer dots, not right on them. When you come to a seam, pick up the dots both sides leaving the seam free. Work the smocking.

To make the garment

Gather the front skirt and join it to the yoke. Baste the smocked panel to the back yoke and sew together by hand as described under the heading "Making the top" in Embroidery chapter 23, page 448. Join back and fronts together at side seams. Stitch the shoulder seams together. Bind the neck edge. Finish by sewing snap fasteners to close the yoke. Join top sleeve to under sleeve, matching notches as indicated on the pattern. Gather the top of the sleeve as indicated on the pattern and make a pleat at sleeve underarm as shown in the diagram. Set the sleeves into the armholes and stitch. Make a small hem at the wrist and thread with elastic. Stitch a narrow hem down front edges and along hem of negligee. Make two bows for wrists, and one with streamers 18 inches long for front neck edge. Sew in position as in diagram.

▼ *The pattern layout reverse one front yoke pattern for one-sided fabric*

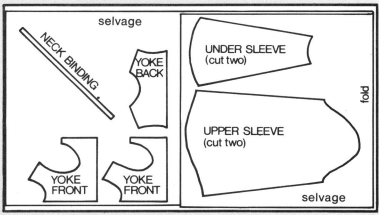

Collector's Piece

Rear Window

This appliqué and needle-point wall panel is a good example of the brilliant effect which can be achieved when a designer breaks the conventions of embroidery. The background stripes are worked in various textured needlepoint stitches using

tones of purple and pink yarns and then the blue shape, representing the mirror frame, has been cut out of matte wool fabric and applied to the needlepoint with invisible stitches. The dullness of the blue enhances the mass of needlepoint in the central circular shape and forms a barrier between that

and the striped stitching of the outer background. The central panel, which represents the view seen in the driving mirror through the rear window of a car, has been freely worked; the stitches are not confined to separate shapes but run into each other and overlap. The art lies in keeping the free

effect without a jumbled mess resulting. Many of the stitches in the central panel vary within themselves as a result of the embroiderer using different textured threads of similar colors, by her changing the direction of a line of stitches or by the varying angles of the stitches themselves.

A soft case for jewelry

This handy little jewelry case is ideal for traveling. With three pockets and a strap to hold rings and earrings, it will carry your jewelry safely and neatly.

Suitable fabrics
Heavy silk, velvet or fine corduroy are all suitable for the covering of the jewelry case. Fine suede or leather wear extremely well and would be very luxurious.

You will need
For pattern making:
- [ ] Graph paper (1in squares)
- [ ] Pencil
- [ ] Scissors

For the case:
- [ ] $\frac{3}{8}$yd 36in wide fabric for the covering
- [ ] $\frac{3}{8}$yd 36in wide muslin for the interlining
- [ ] $\frac{3}{8}$yd 36in wide rayon lining fabric
- [ ] Matching sewing thread, basting thread
- [ ] $\frac{1}{4}$yd $\frac{1}{2}$in wide black leather strip or ribbon for the strap
- [ ] 1 small, 1 large snap fastener
- [ ] $\frac{1}{2}$yd 2in wide decorative braid
- [ ] Rubber cement
- [ ] 6 inch ruler
- [ ] Sharp pointed scissors
- [ ] Three 6in zippers to match the covering fabric

▼ *A useful and attractive traveling jewelry case*

Making the pattern
Copy the pattern shape and its markings from the graph below onto the graph paper, one square on the graph being equal to one 1 inch square on the paper.
Cut out the paper pattern.

The muslin interlining
Pin the paper pattern onto single muslin.
Cut out the muslin around the edge of the pattern. Mark all the placings for zipper openings with basting thread. This is piece A.
Unpin the pattern, repin it to the remaining muslin and cut out another muslin shape, but this time cut $\frac{1}{8}$ inch away from the edge of the pattern (there are no markings on this piece of muslin). This is piece B.

Sticking the muslin to the covering fabric
Cut out the zipper openings accurately on piece A (figure **1**). Remove the basting.

▼ *Graph for the jewelry case pattern, without seam allowance*

ZIPPER OPENING

C   Pocket stitching line   D

●   LEATHER STRAP (position of)

Snap fastener

ZIPPER OPENING

A   Pocket stitching line   B

ZIPPER OPENING

1 square = 1 inch

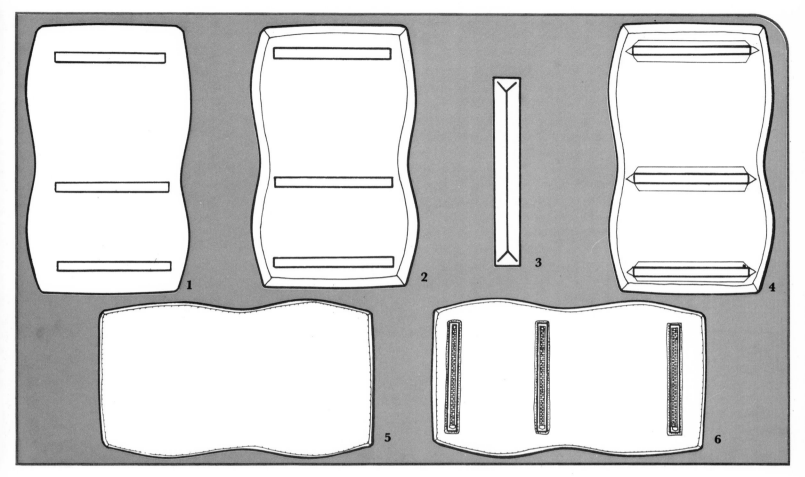

Spread the rubber cement thinly and evenly onto piece A, using the ruler as a spatula. Place the glued side of the muslin onto the wrong side of the uncut covering fabric allowing at least $\frac{1}{2}$ inch of fabric to show all around the muslin. Smooth the muslin down so that there are no air pockets between the layers.

Stick muslin piece B onto the remaining uncut covering fabric in the same way.

Cutting out the covering fabric

Cut out the covering fabric around each muslin piece adding $\frac{1}{2}$ inch turning allowance.

Spread rubber cement onto the turnings and stick them down onto the muslin, snipping into the curves as necessary (figure 2). Allow both pieces to dry and then mark with basting thread on the covering fabric of piece A the cut out zipper openings, the pocket stitching lines and the placing for the strap. Cut out the zipper openings on the covering fabric of piece A as shown in figure 3, and glue the turnings down onto the muslin (figure 4).

Allow this to dry and then stitch in the zippers either by machine or hand, with the right side of the zippers on the covering fabric side of piece A.

Lining

Place both pieces of covered muslin onto the single lining fabric and cut out the lining to the same shape, allowing $\frac{1}{2}$ inch turning on each piece.

Turn under the edges of each lining piece a little over the $\frac{1}{2}$ inch turning allowance, baste down and press carefully. Place a lining piece over each covered muslin piece and slip stitch into place (figure 5). Remove the basting and cut slits in the lining of piece A for the zipper openings as shown in figure 3. Turn under the edges of the lining at the zipper openings and slip stitch into place (figure 6).

The leather strap

Prepare the strip of leather or ribbon by folding under one end and sewing on the ball half of the small snap fastener, securing the turned under end (you can hide the stitches on the right side with a small patch glued into position). Trim and turn under the other end to make it neat, then, working on the right side of piece A, place the strap in position where marked and machine stitch the turned under end down.

Sew the socket half of the small snap fastener onto the covering fabric of piece A so that it will close with the ball half on the strap without strain.

Assembling the case

Place pieces A and B together, linings facing, and pin at the corners. Since piece B is slightly larger than piece A, the extra fabric will have to be eased in as you sew the pieces together; this is so that the case will fold easily without straining at the edges. Baste the pieces together loosely and then, using a fine needle and a double thickness of thread, sew them together by hand, using a firm slip stitch which will be invisible on the surface.

Making the pockets

Machine stitch or firmly back stitch the two pieces together along lines A to B and C to D where marked.

Decoration

Place the strip of decorative braid down the center of piece B and baste. Turn under the ends of the braid to make them neat and then hem stitch the braid into position, being sure to sew only through piece B.

Sew each half of the large snap fastener to the braid, 2 inches from each end.

Dress-making 57

Fine tucks make fine fashion

Tucking is one of the traditional ways of decorating both men's and women's clothes. It gives a well thought out, expensive looking finish to any garment, and lends itself particularly well to simple, easy to make patterns, transforming the design into something special.

As an example, a classic front buttoned shirtdress from Butterick has been taken and tucks have been added down the front and back. The photograph opposite shows the final effect, and you will see from the line drawing beside the photograph that the Center Back seam on the original pattern has been straightened and cut on the fabric fold. The dress is made in Viyella which is an ideal fabric for the beginner to learn the technique of tucking.

As you read through this chapter you will notice illustrations of other Vogue and Butterick patterns which have been selected to show ways in which tucks can be used, on yokes, cuffs, bibs, sleeves and blouse fronts. It must be clearly stated that Creative Hands has superimposed the lines of tucking on the areas mentioned for the purpose of illustrating a point.

Simple tucking is within the capability of every home dressmaker—it only needs a bit of practice. This chapter outlines the principles of tucking so that you can apply the basic technique to the particular garment you wish to make. Many sewing machines have attachments which can be used to make tucking easy, but in this case it is the feel for tucking and practice which makes perfect.

About tucking

Suitable fabrics

Tucks are always made with the grain line since tucking on the bias grain is almost impossible. So the beginner should start on a fabric with an obvious grain line. Alternatively, some pure silks can be thread drawn for the distance of the tucks and the lines of the drawn threads are then used as fold lines for the tucks.

However, concentrating on grain lines can be slightly hypnotic and takes the eye away from other important features, such as the straightness of the stitching lines and the width and distance of the tucks. If you are concentrating only on one single part of the job the stitching lines will suffer and become crooked. So you must learn to feel the grain line rather than always be looking at it. When this feeling has been developed try your hand at crêpe, which has an obscured grain line, and you will see how easy it is to tuck.

It is important that the fabric you choose is easy to press and will take a sharp crease line. Fabrics which are crease resistant must be tested for tucking as they may not allow you to press the tucks in position.

Width of tucking

The width you make the tucks is related to the fabric which is being tucked, but you do have some choice as to the width.

Everyone has seen bad tucking where the tucks stand up from the fabric and the lines are wavy. This is due to the fact that either the wrong size tucks have been made or that the fabric is not suitable for tucking.

Any width of tuck may be used for fine fabrics but be careful with heavier fabrics, they may be suitable only for wide tucks.

Fine tucking should only be applied to short runs such as on bodices, yokes, sleeves or inserts. For longer runs, such as down the length of dress fronts and backs, use wider tucking.

There is also the type of tucking which ends in pleats. Here each tuck fold covers the stitching line of the previous tuck giving the impression of pleating. This type is particularly attractive on a dress when the stitching ends at the hipline, and you have the added advantage of released fullness in the skirt.

Deciding the width

Fine tucking is difficult to gauge, since it varies with the type of fabric you are using. Tucking which looks fine in one fabric can look coarse in another. So on some fabrics you may have to stitch just along the foldline, leaving only one or two grains of the fabric between the stitches and the fold, while on other fabrics you may be able to stitch as wide as four grains from the fold and still have a fine row of tucks as a result.

It is best to test on a scrap of fabric by making several rows of tucking in different widths. Press the tucking and then decide which width is the most suitable.

Wide tucking should be tested in the same way.

How much to tuck

Once you have decided to tuck a garment do not skimp by making too few rows. Tucking looks best in lots of evenly spaced rows or several groups of three or more rows.

Tucking on a dress plays an important part in the overall design of the garment and requires thought.

On dresses with a Center Front, or simulated fastening, start the tucking just beside the fastening, tab or otherwise, and take it across the front until it runs just over the point of the bust on each side (figure **1**).

Tucking confined to the Center Front line makes the front look too wide.

The tucks must not interfere with the fitting detail of a garment, so mark out the darts and end the rows of tucking before you get to the darts. This way you can stitch them without interference and obtain a smooth line.

Another important thing to remember with tucks is the weight they create. Dresses which are only tucked along the front without any compensating weight in the back of the dress tend to drag toward the front. To counteract this you must make the same number of tucks at the back (see back and front views of Viyella dress).

The distance between the tucks

While considering the area and depth of the tucking you must also decide on the distance between the tucks.

Here is a guide to suitable spacing: for fine tucks leave $\frac{1}{2}$ inch to $\frac{5}{8}$ inch between the rows (figure **2**).

For wide tucks it is necessary to test the distance on a scrap of fabric to see where the tucks create bulk. Start making them the same distance apart as they are deep (figure **3**). Press them, and if they look too wide apart try closing them together. Press again, and see what the result is. If they are too close together they will not lie flat after pressing and will always tend to lift a little.

▲ *The Butterick classic shirtdress.*
Right, with tucking added ▶

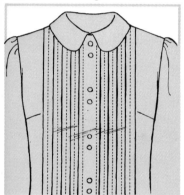

▲ **1.** *Tucking from tab to bust point*

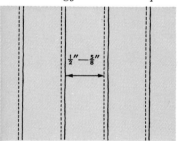

▲ **2.** *Spacing for fine tucks*
▼ **3.** *Tucking spaced to tuck width*

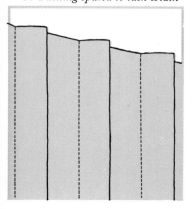

▲ *This dress from Vogue Patterns features wide fitted waist inset, ideal for tucks*

▲ *Here the upper sleeve of a Vogue dress is tucked, and wide tucked belt made to match*

▲ *This softly belted Vogue dress has the yoke emphasized with rows of wide tucks*

Stitching tucks

Carefully test the stitch setting on the machine and make sure that the tension is even. The stitches are an important feature of tucking and may be quite prominent.

For pure or artificial silks use a pure silk sewing thread which will give the rows of stitches an attractive pearl-like appearance. For other fabrics use sewing thread of an appropriate thickness and fiber.

When pinning the tucks, do not use too many pins because as you insert the pin you can roll the folded edge over by as little as a grain and the result will be a tuck which twists.

Always stitch from the top of the tuck; that is, the side which is uppermost after pressing. This means that you must decide beforehand on the direction in which the tucks are to be pressed.

Pressing tucks

A row of tucks straight across the width of a section such as a yoke, is pressed from right to left (figure **4**).

Tucks which are made on either side of a front or back fastening must be pressed to face outward from the center (see figure **1**). To press tucks in position, pin the tucked section on the ironing board, right side up, and gently stretch it as you pin it down until the tucks stand at right angles to the pinned fabric.

Lay a press cloth over the tucks and lightly press them in the direction they are to go. Unpin the fabric and turn it wrong side

up. Lay it on a soft blanket or press cloth and gently press the rows of tucks on the wrong side of the fabric.

Do not force the stitching lines open so that you can see the stitches, but allow the fabric to fold back over them in a sharp crease. Forcing the stitching lines open will distort the tucks on the right side of the fabric. Consequently, they will look uneven and change the direction in which they are to go.

The fabric allowances

When calculating the amount of fabric to allow for a tuck it is not enough to just double the required tuck width, because extra fabric is taken up in the tuck fold and the stitching line. The amount to allow varies with the thickness of the fabric, as follows:

On fabrics which press easily, such as silk, allow double the width of the tuck for the tuck itself and add $\frac{1}{8}$ inch ease to the tuck distance for each row of tucks. This $\frac{1}{8}$ inch will be taken up in the fold of the stitching line (figure **5**).

For firmer and more crease resistant fabrics you will need a little more allowance. Work out the tuck and tuck distance as above then, on the seam allowance, allow an additional $\frac{1}{8}$ inch for every two rows of tucks (figure **6**).

For wide tucking in heavier fabrics allowance has to be made for the tuck fold. Add $\frac{1}{8}$ inch ease to the tuck distance for each row of tucks as above. Then, for the tuck itself, allow double the tuck width

plus $\frac{1}{4}$ inch for each tuck. When stitching the tuck, stitch just inside the seamline and the tuck will come to the desired width (figure **7**).

Preparing a pattern for tucking

Fine tucks on small sections

Taking a bodice as an example, on the pattern measure out the tuck distances starting with a line parallel to the Center Front or Center Back (figure **8**). If you want a distance of $\frac{1}{2}$ inch or so to show clearly between each tuck, add the width of the stitched tuck to this measurement because the distance will be reduced by the tuck width once the tuck has been pressed in position.

Pin the Center Front or Center Back to the straight edge of a sheet of paper and square off the pattern (figure **9a**).

Count the number of tucks, double the width of each tuck and multiply by the number. To this measurement, add the required ease for each tuck, as given above, then add this to the widest part of the pattern (figure **9b**).

Also add 1 inch for seam allowance all around (figure **9c**) and cut out along these lines. Use this oblong as a pattern to cut out the fabric.

Tuck the fabric then, using the original pattern, cut out the tucked fabric to the correct shape.

Use this squaring off method on blouses,

leaving the cutting out of the neckline, shoulder and armhole shapes until the tucks have been stitched and pressed. Do not be tempted to cut the sloping seams before tucking, since on many fabrics you will lose control over the straight of the grain when you come to the end of each tuck, and this can cause distortion.

Wide tucks on long sections

To prepare a pattern for wide tucks, especially on long sections of a garment, the tucking allowances must be included in the pattern before cutting, and the pattern must be worked out with great precision.

This pattern is not squared off as before—the shapes are cut out before tucking. Start by pinning the Center Front or Center Back of the pattern to the straight edge of a sheet of paper and work as shown below. To simplify the calculations $\frac{1}{2}$ inch tucks are used here at $\frac{1}{2}$ inch intervals. For different size tucks simply substitute that measurement for the $\frac{1}{2}$ inch. For tucks facing away from the center lines measure out the width of a plain center panel. Then measure out the distances between the tucks, $\frac{1}{2}$ inch distance plus $\frac{1}{2}$ inch for the previous tuck fold, so making the lines one inch apart. Draw pencil lines parallel to the center lines on these measurements (figure **10a**).

Cut the pattern on the first pencil line and spread the cut sections to make the first tuck row. The spreading should be $1\frac{1}{8}$ inch to allow for ease. Pin the pattern down securely.

Cut and spread the remaining pattern in the same way (figure **10b**).

To make the new pattern, draw around the outline of the spread pattern. Then draw along the front edge of each cut section to mark the distances of the tucks (figure **10b**).

To mark the tuck fold lines, measure $\frac{1}{2}$ inch from each pencil line and draw a straight line parallel to the cut edge (figure **10b**). Cut out the new pattern.

If the dress has a plain Center Front

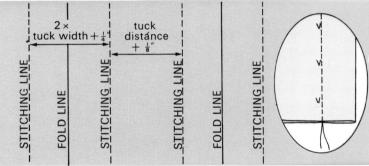

▲ **4.** *Tucks pressed from right to left on yoke section*

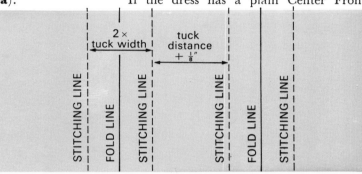

▲ **5.** *Allowance of $\frac{1}{8}$ inch on tuck distance for easily pressed fabrics*

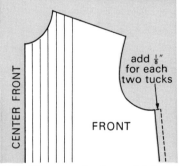

▲ **6.** *Allowance for firmer fabrics*

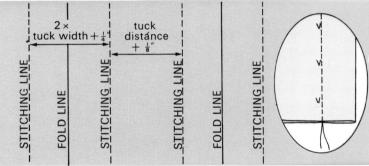

▲ **7.** *Allowances and stitching tucks on heavier fabrics*

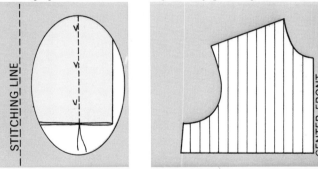

▲ **8.** *Marking fine tucks*

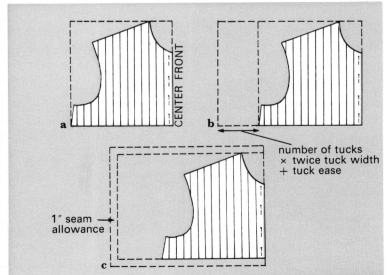

▲ **9.** *Fine tucks on small areas:* **a.** *squaring off the pattern;* **b.** *adding tucking allowances at the widest part;* **c.** *adding 1 inch seam allowance all round*

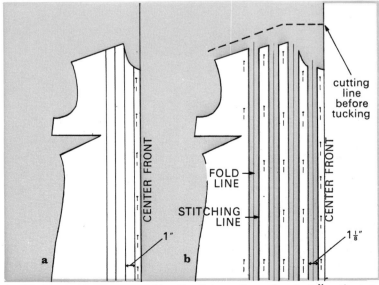

▲ **10.** *Long tuck run:* **a.** *marking the distance lines;* **b.** *spreading the pattern, marking the front edge of each cut section and the stitching lines*

fastening, button-down or invisible, choose a suitable distance from the Center Front line, where the tucking will not interfere with the edge of the wrap when the dress is fastened, and start to mark out the rows for tucks. Then make the new pattern as before.

Tucked front and simulated tab fastening

To make a simulated button bar or tab on a tucked front as shown in figure **11**

is very simple. All you have to do is make a tuck fold the same distance from the Center Front line as the edge of the wrap. Then, after the garment has been made, topstitch along the wrap edge a distance equal to the width of the tucks and the simulated button bar is complete. Since this row of tucking is not repeated on the left side of the dress (figure **12**), to avoid unnecessary thickness it is essential that you make a right and left Front pattern piece.

Making the right Front pattern for $\frac{1}{2}$ inch tucking (figure **12**). Measure the distance from the wrap edge to the Center Front and use the measurement to find the fold line for the first row of tucks, which becomes the inside edge of the tab.

Draw a pencil line on the pattern and mark it fold line.

To measure out the succeeding tuck folds, start from the fold line of the tab and measure out distances of 1 inch.

Pin the pattern to the straight edge of a sheet of paper to make a new pattern, and cut through the pencil fold lines.

Spread each cut section $1\frac{1}{8}$ inch and mark in stitching lines $\frac{1}{2}$ inch from the folds.

Making the left Front pattern (figure **12**). Exclude the marking of the fold line for the inner tab edge and copy the lines for the tucking, starting with the second row of tucks.

To complete the Front patterns, attach a front facing pattern to each Front to avoid cutting separate facings and thereby adding seams to the wrap edges (figure **13**).

Layout, cutting, marking

Layout and cutting notes

When you make the layout for a tucked garment make slightly deeper allowances for the seam edges, since some allowances need tidying up after the tucks have been stitched.

Marking for wide tucks

Tailor's tack the stitching line for tuck distance and along the fold line.

Remove the pattern and crease the fabric on the fold line of the tuck. Pin the folded edge lightly, spacing the pins at approximately 10 inch intervals. Test for the straight of the grain and adjust if the pins or markings have slipped out of the grain line.

Mark out $\frac{1}{2}$ inch (or the depth of the tuck) for the stitching line at the beginning of the row, then stitch the tuck and gauge the stitch distance from the folded edge by using the presser foot on the machine as your guide.

Working with a tape measure. Once you have become familiar with tucking you will be able to dispense with tailor's tacking completely and just use a tape measure. Measure out the distances at the beginning of each row, pin the folded edge lightly, then use the foot on your machine to guide you and checking that you have maintained an equal distance along each row.

Marking for narrow tucks

Use the tape measure method given above.

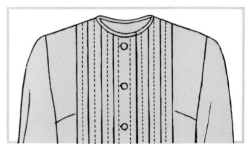

▲ **11.** *Tucked Front giving simulated button bar*

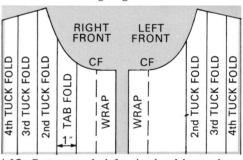

▲ **12.** *Pattern marked for simulated button bar*
▼ **13.** *Attaching the front facing to the Front*

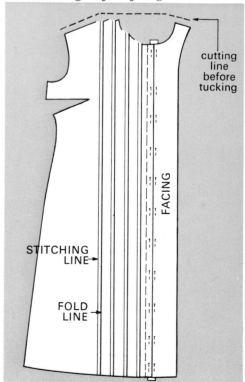

Scarlet spray

This flower spray in shadow appliqué has been worked by applying scarlet lawn to white organdy. In some areas, the scarlet lawn is on the wrong side of the fabric, giving a soft pink effect, and in others it is applied to the right side, giving a brilliant contrast. The edges of the applied areas are worked in whipped chain stitch and pin stitch. The outer petals on the central flower are embroidered with diagonal ringed backstitch worked over counted threads, and four-sided stitch has been used on the smaller flowers. The details of the flowers are worked in satin stitch and outline stitch.

Shetland lace baby shawl

Because this shawl has few seams, the amount of finishing is minimal.

Size
About 60in square.

Gauge
About 4 sts and 8 rows to 1in over garter st worked on No.7 needles

Materials
Reynolds Wendy Whisper 16 25 grm balls
One pair No.7 needles (or Canadian No.6)

Outer border

Using No.7 needles, cast on 8 sts.
1st row K2, (ytf, K2 tog) 3 times.
2nd and every other row K.
3rd row K2, ytf, K2 tog, ytf, K2, ytf, K2 tog.
5th row K2, ytf, K2 tog, ytf, K3, ytf, K2 tog.
7th row K2, ytf, K2 tog, ytf, K1, ytf, K2 tog, K1, ytf, K2 tog.
9th row K2, ytf, K2 tog, ytf, K3, (ytf, K2 tog) twice.
11th row K1, (K2 tog, ytf) twice, K3 tog, ytf, K2, ytf, K2 tog.
13th row K1, (K2 tog, ytf) twice, K2 tog, K2, ytf, K2 tog.
15th row K1, (K2 tog, ytf) twice, K2 tog, K1, ytf, K2 tog.
17th row K1, (K2 tog, ytf) 3 times, K2 tog.
18th row K.
Rep 1st—18th rows 21 times more. Bind off.

1142

Main border

Pick up and K181 sts along straight edge of border.
1st row K.
2nd row K2, *K2 tog, ytf, K4, rep from * to last 5 sts, K2 tog, ytf, K3.
3rd and every other row K.
4th row K1, *K2 tog, ytf, K1, ytf, K2 tog, K1, rep from * to end.
6th row K2 tog, ytf, *K3, ytf, K3 tog, ytf, rep from * to last 5 sts, K3, ytf, K2 tog.
8th row K1, *ytf, K2 tog, ytf, K3 tog, ytf, K1, rep from * to end.
10th row K2, *ytf, K3 tog, ytf, K3, rep from * to last 5 sts, ytf, K3 tog, ytf, K2.
12th row K1, K2 tog, ytf, (K1, ytf, K2 tog, ytf, K3 tog, ytf) twice, K7, *(ytf, K2 tog, ytf, K3 tog, ytf, K1) 3 times, K6, rep from * to last 15 sts, (ytf, K2 tog, ytf, K3 tog, ytf, K1) twice, ytf, K2 tog, K1.
14th row K2 tog, ytf, (K3, ytf, K3 tog, ytf) twice, *K2, K2 tog, ytf, K1, ytf, K2 tog, K2, (ytf, K3 tog, ytf, K3) twice, ytf, K3 tog, ytf, rep from * to last 23 sts, K2, K2 tog, ytf, K1, ytf, K2 tog, K2, (ytf, K3 tog, ytf, K3) twice, ytf, K2 tog.
16th row K1, *(ytf, K2 tog, ytf, K3 tog, ytf, K1) twice, K2, K2 tog, ytf, K3, ytf, K2, tog, K3, rep from * to last 12 sts, (ytf, K2 tog, ytf, K3 tog, ytf, K1) twice.
18th row K2, *(ytf, K3 tog, ytf, K3) twice, (K2 tog, ytf) twice, K1, (ytf, K2 tog) twice, K3, rep from * to last 11 sts, ytf, K3 tog, ytf, K3, ytf, K3 tog, ytf, K2.
20th row K1, K2 tog, ytf, K1, *ytf, K2 tog, ytf, K3 tog, ytf, K4, (K2 tog, ytf) twice, K3, (ytf, K2 tog) twice, K4, rep from * to last 9 sts, ytf, K2 tog, ytf, K3 tog, ytf, K1, ytf, K2 tog, K1.
22nd row K2 tog, ytf, *K3, ytf, K3 tog, ytf, K4, (K2 tog, ytf) 3 times, K1, (ytf, K2 tog) 3 times, K1, rep from * to last 11 sts, K3, ytf, K3 tog, ytf, K3, ytf, K2 tog.
24th row K1, ytf, K2 tog, ytf, K3 tog, ytf, K5 (K2 tog, ytf) 3 times, *K3, (ytf, K2 tog) 3 times, K3, K2 tog, ytf, K4 (K2 tog, ytf) 3 times, rep from * to last 20 sts, K3, (ytf, K2 tog) 3 times, K5, ytf, K2 tog, ytf, K3 tog, ytf, K1.
26th row K2, ytf, K3 tog, ytf, K5, (K2 tog, ytf) 4 times, K1, (ytf, K2 tog) 4 times, *K7, (K2 tog, ytf) 4 times, K1, (ytf, K2 tog) 4 times, rep from * to last 10 sts, K5, ytf, K3 tog, ytf, K2.
28th row K1, K2 tog, ytf, K6, (K2 tog, ytf) 4 times, K3, (ytf, K2 tog) 4 times, *K1, K2 tog, ytf, K2, (K2 tog, ytf) 4 times, K3, (ytf, K2 tog) 4 times, rep from * to last 9 sts, K6, ytf, K2 tog, K1.
30th row K2 tog, ytf, K6, *(K2 tog, ytf) 5 times, K1, (ytf, K2 tog) 5 times, K3, rep from * to last 5 sts, K3, ytf, K2 tog.
32nd row K7, *(K2 tog, ytf) 5 times, K3, (ytf, K2 tog) 5 times, K1, rep from * to last 6 sts, K6.
34th row K1, K2 tog, K5, work as 30th row from * to last 5 sts, K2, K2 tog, K1. (179 sts.)
36th row K1, K2 tog, K5, *(K2 tog, ytf) 4 times, K3, (ytf, K2 tog) 4 times, K5, rep from * to last 3 sts, K2 tog, K1. (177 sts.)
38th row K1, K2 tog, K5, *(K2 tog, ytf) 4 times, K1, (ytf, K2 tog) 4 times, K1, K2 tog, ytf, K1, ytf, K2 tog, K1, rep from * to last 25 sts, (K2 tog, ytf) 4 times, K1, (ytf, K2 tog) 4 times, K5, K2 tog, K1. (175 sts.)
40th row K1, K2 tog, K5, *(K2 tog, ytf) 3 times, K3, (ytf, K2 tog) 3 times, K1, K2 tog, ytf, K3, ytf, K2 tog, K1, rep from * to last 23 sts, (K2 tog, ytf) 3 times, K3, (ytf, K2 tog) 3 times, K5, K2 tog, K1. (173 sts.)
42nd row K1, K2 tog, K5, *(K2 tog, ytf) 3 times, K1, (ytf, K2 tog) 3 times, K1, (K2 tog, ytf) twice, K1, (ytf, K2 tog) twice, K1, rep from * to last 21 sts, (K2 tog, ytf) 3 times, K1, (ytf, K2 tog) 3 times, K5, K2 tog, K1. (171 sts.)
44th row K1, K2 tog, K5, *(K2 tog, ytf) twice, K3, (ytf, K2 tog) twice, K1, rep from * to last 7 sts, K4, K2 tog, K1.
46th row K1, K2 tog, K5, *(K2 tog, ytf) twice, K1, (ytf, K2 tog) twice, K1, (K2 tog, ytf) 3 times, K1, (ytf, K2 tog) 3 times, K1, rep from * to last 17 sts, (K2 tog, ytf) twice, K1, (ytf, K2 tog) twice, K5, K2 tog, K1.
48th row K1, K2 tog, K5, *K2 tog, ytf, K3, ytf, K2 tog, K1, (K2 tog, ytf) 3 times, K3, (ytf, K2 tog) 3 times, K1, rep from * to last 15 sts, K2 tog, ytf, K3, ytf, K2 tog, K5, K2 tog, K1.
50th row K1, K2 tog, K5, *K2 tog, ytf, K1, ytf, K2 tog, K1, (K2 tog, ytf) 4 times, K1, (ytf, K2 tog) 4 times, K1, rep from * to last 13 sts, K2 tog, ytf, K1, ytf, K2 tog, K5, K2 tog, K1.
52nd row K1, K2 tog, K6, *ytf, K2 tog, K1, (K2 tog, ytf) 4 times, K3, (ytf, K2 tog) 4 times, K2, rep from * to last 34 sts, ytf, K2 tog, K1, (K2 tog, ytf) 4 times, K3, (ytf, K2 tog) 4 times, K1, K2 tog, ytf, K6, K2 tog, K1.
54th row K1, K2 tog, K7, *(K2 tog, ytf) 5 times, K1, (ytf, K2 tog) 5 times, K3, rep from * to last 7 sts, K4, K2 tog, K1. (159 sts.)
56th row K1, K2 tog, K5, *(K2 tog, ytf) 5 times, K3,

ytf, K2 tog) 5 times, K1,
ep from * to last 7 sts, K4,
K2 tog, K1.

58th row K1, K2 tog, K5,
*(K2 tog, ytf) 5 times, K1,
ytf, K2 tog) 5 times, K3,
ep from * to last 5 sts, K2,
K2 tog, K1.

60th row K1, K2 tog, K5,
*(K2 tog, ytf) 4 times, K3,
ytf, K2 tog) 4 times, K2,
ytf, K2 tog, K1, rep from
* to last 27 sts, (K2 tog, ytf)
4 times, K3, (ytf, K2 tog)
4 times, K5, K2 tog, K1.

62nd row K1, K2 tog, K5,
*(K2 tog, ytf) 4 times, K1,
ytf, K2 tog) 4 times, K2,
ytf, K3 tog, ytf, K2, rep
from * to last 25 sts, (K2 tog,
ytf) 4 times, K1, (ytf,
K2 tog) 4 times, K5, K2 tog,
K1.

64th row K1, K2 tog, K5,
*(K2 tog, ytf) 3 times, K3,
ytf, K2 tog) 3 times, K4,
ytf, K2 tog, K3, rep from
* to last 23 sts, (K2 tog,
ytf) 3 times, K3, (ytf, K2
tog) 3 times, K5, K2 tog, K1.

66th row K1, K2 tog, K5,
*(K2 tog, ytf) 3 times, K1,
ytf, K2 tog) 3 times, K11,
ep from * to last 21 sts, (K2
tog, ytf) 3 times, K1,
ytf, K2 tog) 3 times, K5,
K2 tog, K1. (147 sts.)

68th row K1, K2 tog, K5,
*(K2 tog, ytf) twice, K3,
ytf, K2 tog) twice, K6,
ytf, K2 tog, K5, rep from
* to last 19 sts, (K2 tog, ytf)
twice, K3, (ytf, K2 tog)
twice, K5, K2 tog, K1.

70th row K1, K2 tog, K5,
*(K2 tog, ytf) twice, K1,
ytf, K2 tog) twice, K5, K2
tog, ytf, K1, ytf, K2 tog,
K5, rep from * to last 17 sts,
(K2 tog, ytf) twice, K1,
(ytf, K2 tog) twice, K5, K2
tog, K1.

72nd row K1, K2 tog, K5,
*K2 tog, ytf, K3, ytf, K2
tog, K5, rep from * to last
3 sts, K2 tog, K1.

74th row K1, K2 tog, K5,
*K2 tog, ytf, K1, ytf, K2
tog, K4, K2 tog, ytf, K1,
ytf, K2 tog, ytf, K3 tog,
ytf, K1, ytf, K2 tog, K4,
ep from * to last 13 sts, K2
tog, ytf, K1, ytf, K2 tog,
K5, K2 tog, K1.

76th row K1, K2 tog, K5,

▲ *A perfect example of openwork stitches and fine yarn combining to make a soft and warm baby shawl*

*K2 tog, ytf, K5, K2 tog,
ytf, K3, ytf, K3 tog, ytf,
K3, ytf, K2 tog, K4, rep
from * to last 11 sts, K2 tog,
ytf, K6, K2 tog, K1.

78th row K1, K2 tog, K9,
*K2 tog, ytf, (K1, ytf,
K2 tog, K3 tog, ytf)
twice, K1, ytf, K2 tog, K7,
rep from * to last 5 sts, K2,
K2 tog, K1.

80th row K1, K2 tog, K7,
*K2 tog, ytf, (K3, ytf,
K3 tog, ytf) twice, K3,
ytf, K2 tog, K5, rep from
* to last 5 sts, K2, K2 tog,
K1.

82nd row K1, K2 tog, K4,
*K2 tog, ytf, (K1, ytf,
K2 tog, K3 tog, ytf)
3 times, K1, ytf, K2 tog,
K1, rep from * to last 6 sts,
K3, K2 tog, K1.

84th row K1, K2 tog, K2,
K2 tog, *ytf, K3, ytf,
K3 tog, rep from * to last
10 sts, ytf, K3, ytf, K2
tog, K2, K2 tog, K1. (129 sts.)

86th row K1, K2 tog, K2,

*ytf, K2 tog, ytf, K3 tog,
ytf, K1, rep from * to last
4 sts, K1, K2 tog, K1.

88th row K1, K2 tog, K2,
*ytf, K3 tog, ytf, K3,
rep from * to last 8 sts, ytf,
K3 tog, ytf, K2, K2 tog, K1.

90th row K5, *ytf, K2 tog,
K4, rep from * to last 6sts,
ytf, K2 tog, K4. (125 sts.)

91st row K.
Bind off loosely.
Work one more outer border
and main border in the same
way.
Make a third section in the
same way, either binding off
or leaving the sts on a holder
to be woven to last row of
center. Make a fourth section
but do not bind off,
continuing on these 125 sts
for center.

Center

1st-8th rows K.

9th row K8, *ytf, K2 tog,
K4, rep from * to last 3 sts,
K3.

10th and every other row K.

11th row K7, *ytf, K3 tog,
ytf, K3, rep from * to last
4 sts, K4.

13th row As 9th.

15th row K.

17th row K8, ytf, K2 tog,
K to last 9 sts, ytf, K2 tog,
K7.

19th row K7, ytf, K3 tog,
ytf, K to last 10 sts, ytf,
K3 tog, ytf, K7.

21st row As 17th.

23rd row K.
Rep last 8 rows 27 times more,
then rep 9th-14th rows once.
K8 rows more.
Bind off loosely or weave to
last border section.

Finishing

Slip stitch border sections to
center sides. Slip stitch
corners together. Roll in a
damp towel for 2 hours. Pin
to measurement with rust-proof
pins; allow to dry.

Contrasting colored two-piece dress

The unusual waist detail of the pullover top with its shaped point makes this a particularly slimming and effective two-piece dress.

Sizes

Directions are for 32in bust with 34in hips.
Pullover length to center back, 18[18½:19:19½]in. Sleeve seam, 4in.
Skirt length, 21[21½:22:22½] in, adjustable.
The figures in brackets [] refer to the 34, 36 and 38in bust sizes with 36, 38 and 40in hips, respectively.

Gauge

6 sts and 8 rows to 1in over st st worked on No.5 needles.

Materials

Sports Yarn
Pullover 4[4:5:5] 2oz skeins of main color A
Skirt 3[4:4:4] 2oz skeins of contrast color B
1 2oz skein of main color A
One pair No.3 needles (or Canadian No.10)
One pair No.5 needles (or Canadian No.8)

Pullover 5in zipper and 1 button
Skirt 7in zipper and waist length of elastic

Skirt (back and front)

Using No.3 needles and B, cast on 78[84:90:96] sts. Work 1¼in garter st, ending with a WS row.
Change to No.5 needles. Beg with a K row, work 4 rows st st.
Next row K24[26:28:30] sts, inc 1 by picking up loop between sts and K tbl, K2, inc 1, K26[28:30:32] sts, inc 1, K2, inc 1, K to end.
Beg with a P row, work 7 rows without shaping.
Next row K25[27:29:31] sts, inc 1, K2, inc 1, K28[30:32: 34] sts, inc 1, K2, inc 1, K to end.
Beg with a P row, work 7 rows without shaping.
Continue in this way, inc in next and every following 8th row until there are 130 [136:142:148] sts.
Continue without shaping until work measures 19¼ [20:20½:21]in, or 1½in less than desired length, ending with a P row.
Change to No.3 needles. Attach A and K 12 rows.
With B, work 2 rows st st. With A, K 11 rows.
Using a No.5 needle, bind off loosely k-wise.

Pullover

Back

Using No.3 needles and A, cast on 82[88:94:100] sts. Work 10 rows garter st.
Change to No.5 needles. Beg with a K row, continue in st st, inc one st at each end of 7th and every following 8th row until there are 100 [106:112:118] sts.
Continue without shaping until work measures 11½in from beg, ending with a P row.

Shape armholes

Bind off 4 sts at beg of next 2 rows, then 2 sts at beg of next 2 rows.
**Next row K1, sl 1, K1, psso, K to last 3 sts, K2 tog, K1.

Next row P to end.**
Rep last 2 rows 6]7:8:9] times more. 74[78:82:86] sts.
Continue without shaping until armholes measure 2½[3:3½:4]in, ending with a P row.

Divide for opening

Next row K37[39:41:43] sts, turn. Slip rem sts on holder.
Next row K2, P to end.
Next row K to end.
Rep last 2 rows until armhole measures 6½[7:7½:8]in from beg, ending with a P row.

Shape shoulder

At arm edge, bind off 7[7:8:8] sts every other row twice, then 6[7:6:7] sts once.
Bind off rem 17[18:19:20] sts. With RS facing, attach yarn to sts on holder, K to end.
Next row P to last 2 sts, K2. Complete to correspond to first side.

Front

Using No.3 needles and A, cast on 92[98:104:110] sts.
1st row K to end.
2nd row K57[61:65:69] sts, K2 tog, K1, K2 tog tbl, K to end.
3rd row K to end.
4th row K56[60:64:68]sts, K2 tog, K1, K2 tog tbl, K to end.
5th row K to end.
Continue to dec in this way on next and every other row 3 times more. 82[88:94:100] sts.
Change to No.5 needles.
Next row K to end.
Next row P57[61:65:69] sts, turn.
Next row Sl 1, K4, turn.
Next row Sl 1, P8, turn.
Next row Sl 1, K14, turn.
Next row Sl 1, P18, turn.
Next row Sl 1, K24, turn.
Continue in this way working 4 more sts on every P row and 6 more sts on every K row until there are 55[55:65:65] sts on needle in work, ending with a K row.
Next row P to end.
Next row K to end.
Beg with a P row, continue in st st, inc one st at each end of 4th and every following 8th row until there are 100[106:

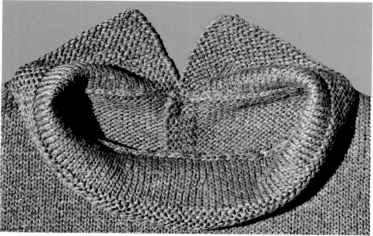

▲ *Close-up of collar*
▼ *Close-up of shaped point and button*

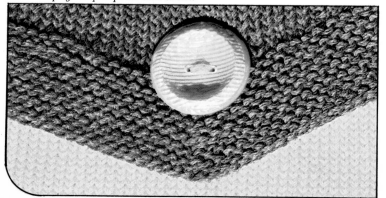

112:118] sts.
Continue without shaping
until side edge measures same
as back to underarm, ending
with a P row.

Shape armholes

Same as given for back.
Continue without shaping
until armholes measure 4½[5:
5½:6]in from beg, ending with
a K row.
Next row P31[32:33:34] sts,
bind off 12[14:16:18] sts, P to
end.
Complete this side first.

Shape neck

K1 row.
At neck edge, bind off 3 sts;
then 2 sts every other row
twice.
Dec one st at neck edge on
every other row until 20[21:
22:23] sts rem.
Continue without shaping
until armhole measures same
as back to shoulder, ending
with a P row.

Shape shoulder

At arm edge, bind off 7[7:8:8]
sts every other row twice, then
6[7:6:7] sts once.
With RS of work facing,
attach yarn to rem sts and
complete to match first side.

Sleeves

Using No.3 needles and A,
cast on 65[67:69:71] sts.
Work 10 rows garter st.
Change to No.5 needles.
Beg with a K row, continue in
st st, inc one st at each end of
next and every 4th row until
there are 73[75:77:79] sts.
Continue without shaping
until sleeve measures 4in from
beg, ending with a P row.

Shape cap

Bind off 4 sts at beg of next
2 rows.
Rep from ** to ** as given
for Back until 47 sts rem.
Bind off 2 sts at beg of next
10 rows; 3 sts at beg of next
4 rows; then 4 sts at beg of
next 2 rows.
Bind off rem 7 sts.

Collar

Using No.5 needles and A,
cast on 96[100:104:108] sts.

▲ *The contrast band of garter stitch on the skirt hemline links with the top, achieving an all-in-one effect*

Work 10 rows garter st.
Beg with a K row, work 4
rows st st, keeping 6 sts at
each end in garter st.
Next row K7[9:6:8] sts,
(K2 tog, K8) 8[8:9:9] times,
K2 tog, K7[9:6:8] sts.
Work 1 row.
Change to No.3 needles and
continue in st st, keeping 6 sts

at each end in garter st, until
work measures 3in from beg,
ending with a K row. Bind
off k-wise.

Finishing

Press each piece under a damp
cloth with a warm iron.
Skirt Join side seams leaving

left seam open for zipper. Sew
in zipper. Join elastic into
circle; sew inside waistband
using casing st. Press seams.
Pullover Join shoulder, side
and sleeve seams. Sew in
sleeves. Sew on collar. Sew in
zipper. Press seams. Sew on
button to beg of st st just
above point at lower edge.

Loopy crochet makes a stole

Although very effective, the technique of working crochet loops is simple and quick. The stole pattern incorporates both openwork and looped fringing rows.

The technique used for looping stitches in crochet makes it possible to create openwork rows of any depth desired or, alternatively, to work rows of loops into the actual crochet to form fringing. The same fringing worked all over the fabric creates a fluffy fur-like surface.

Working openwork rows

This effect is worked by pulling a long loop the desired length out of a simple single crochet all along one row and then working the tips of the loops together on the following row with single crochet.

Several rows may then be worked before another openwork row is made or, alternatively, a very lacy fabric can be achieved by working openwork rows on every other row. To make a swatch, ch20.

1st row Work 1sc into 2nd ch from hook, *1sc into next ch, rep from * to end. Turn.

2nd row Ch1, *1sc into next st, rep from * to end.

3rd row As 2nd.

4th row Insert hook into first st, yrh and draw through 1 loop on hook, yrh and draw through both loops and drawing the new loop out to the desired length, *insert hook into next st, yrh, draw through 1 loop, yrh, draw through long loop pulling it up to the desired length, slip hook out of loop and rep from * to end of row. It may be found that it is easier to keep the loop on the hook until several are made so that it is simpler to keep them the same length.

5th row Work a number of chains the same length as the loop, insert hook into top of loop, yrh, draw through 1 loop, yrh and draw through both loops, * insert hook into next loop, yrh and draw through 1 loop, yrh and draw through both loops, rep from * along row to end.

Work several rows sc before repeating 4th row as required.

Fringing

Fringing can be worked over the fingers, but is more even when the length of loops is controlled by a piece of cardboard cut to the desired depth. Before beginning to crochet, cut a piece of cardboard, strong enough not to bend, to the desired depth and long enough to hold easily. It is not necessary to have the cardboard the full length of a row. Several loops can be worked and then the cardboard moved along.

To make a swatch, cut a piece of cardboard 1in deep and 6in long. Ch20.

Work 2 rows sc. Turn.

3rd row Hold cardboard in left hand, the base even with top of previous row. Take yarn over top of cardboard and down behind the cardboard. Insert the hook into the first st and draw yarn from the back through 1 loop, yrh and draw through both loops, rep from * to end of row. Turn. Remove the cardboard.

4th row Ch1, 1sc into each st. Work next row as 3rd row or if a shorter fringe is desired, work several rows sc before again working a loop row.

Long, dainty fringes can be worked by cutting a deep piece of cardboard and spacing the rows an inch or more apart. Short, thick, furlike fringes can be made by working over a narrow cardboard with thick yarn and working every alternate row as fringe.

Looped stole

Size

Approx 23in wide by 76in long.

Materials

3-ply fingering yarn—
9 ounces
One No.F (4.00 mm) crochet hook
One piece stiff cardboard 2in deep by 8in long

Stole

Cut the cardboard to the desired depth of fringing before beginning to crochet. Ch96.

1st row Into 2nd ch from hook work 1sc, *1sc into next ch, rep from * to end. Turn.

2nd row Ch1, *1sc into next sc, rep from * to end. Turn.

3rd row As 2nd.

4th row (WS and fringe row) Ch1, *hold cardboard behind and above work, the base even with top of last row, take yarn up and over top of cardboard and down behind it, insert hook into next st and draw loop of yarn from behind base of cardboard through one st, yrh and draw through both loops, rep from * to end.

5th row As 2nd.

Rep 4th and 5th rows 10 times more.

Continue in openwork patt. Work 2 rows sc as 2nd row of fringe.

3rd row Draw loop on hook out to ½in long, *insert hook into next sc, yrh and draw through one st, yrh and draw through both loops until ½in long, leave loop on crochet hook until a few sts have been worked or slip it off and continue with next st as preferred, rep from * to last st, work ss into last st, ch4. Turn.

4th row Loop of last ch on hook, *insert hook into top of next long loop, yrh and draw through one st, yrh and draw through both loops, rep from * to end.

5th and 6th rows Work all sts in sc.

Rep 3rd, 4th, 5th and 6th rows once.

11th, 12th, 13th and 14th rows Work in sc.

Rep 3rd, 4th, 5th and 6th rows twice.

Rep last 18 rows until work measures 38in. Fasten off ends. Work a second piece in the same way. Slip stitch both pieces together.

▼ Working the loops together after an openwork row

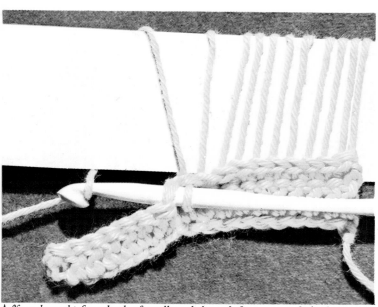

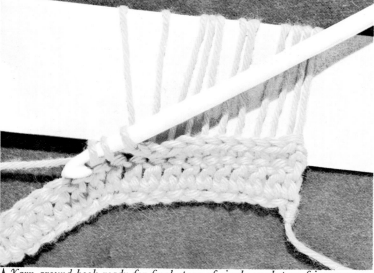

▲ *Yarn brought from back of cardboard through first stage of single crochet*
A fine stole worked in a combination of openwork rows and fringing ▶

▲ *Yarn around hook ready for final stage of single crochet on fringe row*
▼ *The looped fringe when the cardboard has been removed*

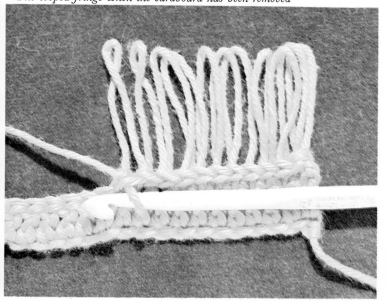

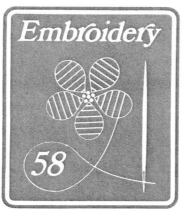

Embroidery

58

The technique of shadow appliqué

So far, when working appliqué, emphasis has been placed on using simple shapes and firm fabrics. In shadow appliqué, the effect is achieved by combining strong colors and sheer or semi-sheer fabrics. The charming flower motifs in this chapter have been worked by applying a bright scarlet lawn to white organdy. This type of appliqué can be used on tablecloths, curtains, and bedspreads, and looks particularly pretty on bed linen. For stunning fashion embroidery, work a motif on the pocket of a sheer organza blouse, and a wedding dress would look magnificent decorated with an all-over pattern of sprays in self-colored appliqué.

The technique of shadow appliqué is one where a transparent or semi-transparent fabric, such as lawn, is decoratively applied to another transparent fabric, such as organdy or voile. The colors can match or contrast and for interesting effects printed fabrics can be used.

Working shadow appliqué

To prepare for embroidery, trace the design onto the wrong side of the background fabric. Baste the two layers of fabric together, using small stitches and following the outline of the design. For delicate floral motifs, such as those in this chapter, only the petals and leaf shapes are worked in appliqué; stems and small leaf shapes are embroidered after the appliqué work is finished.

Using a fine thread, such as coton à broder or two strands of six-strand floss, embroider the outlines of the design following the basting line. Pin stitch, chain stitch or whipped chain stitch can be used for outlining.

Decide whether the contrasting fabric is to be applied to the right side of the design for brilliant contrast or to the wrong side for a softer, pastel effect.

For small motifs such as those given in this chapter, shadow appliqué can be worked in the hand. For larger pieces, a small frame or hoop can be used.

When the applied parts of the design have been completed, cut away the surplus fabric with very sharp, pointed scissors. Cut close to the embroidery. Complete the design by working flower details, stems and small leaves in complementary stitches.

Complementary stitches

The stitches used to complement the appliqué motifs are worked over counted threads, such as ringed backstitch, diagonal ringed backstitch and four-sided stitch.

Other surface stitches, such as satin stitch, chain stitch, whipped chain stitch, buttonhole stitch and outline stitch, are used for the details and give a rich, raised texture.

▼ *The festive effect of a tablecloth worked with sprays of flowers in brilliant scarlet on a white ground*

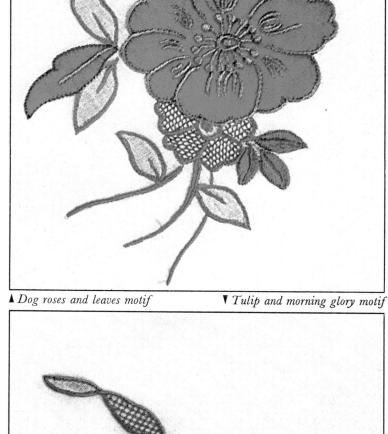

▲ *Tracing pattern for dog rose motif*   ▼ *Tracing pattern for the tulip motif*   ▲ *Dog roses and leaves motif*   ▼ *Tulip and morning glory motif*

Toy making 7

Ram in a thicket

Here are tracing patterns and full directions for making Randy Ram, a curly-headed charmer with a flowing coat!

You will need
For the pattern:
- ☐ Tracing paper
- ☐ Pencil
- ☐ Scissors

For Randy Ram:
- ☐ ¼yd 54in wide firmly woven woolen fabric for the body
- ☐ Two 2oz skeins of Aran knitting yarn for the coat
- ☐ Small pieces of black and white felt for the eyes
- ☐ 12in square of felt or firm fabric for the horns
- ☐ 10oz kapok
- ☐ 10in of ½in wide straight tape
- ☐ Rubber cement
- ☐ Matching sewing thread, basting thread
- ☐ Strip of stiff paper 12in x 2in

Making the pattern
Using the tracing paper, trace all the pattern pieces and their markings from the tracing patterns on pages 1152 and 1153. Cut out the patterns.

Cutting the fabric
Fold the main fabric, right sides facing, and pin the body pattern piece on double fabric and the base and head gusset patterns on single. Make sure that there is at least ½ inch of fabric showing around each pattern piece, and that the grain of the fabric follows the grain lines on the patterns. Cut out 2 body pieces, 1 base and 1 head gusset, adding ½ inch seam allowances.
Mark all the pattern detail with basting thread and also mark around the edge of each pattern piece for the stitching line.
Fold the fabric for the horns, right sides facing, pin the horn pattern piece to the double fabric, and cut out one pair of horns adding seam allowance. Mark the pattern details. Unpin the pattern, repin it to the double fabric, and cut out another pair of horns in exactly the same way.

Making the basic shape
Working on the wrong side of the fabric, machine stitch the dart on each body piece, then place the body pieces together, right sides facing, and stitch from A to B.
Place the head gusset, right sides facing, onto one side of the body, matching B to C and stitch. Repeat this on the other side, stitching the gusset into place, then stitch the body from C to D and E to F. Stitch the base in place, matching F to F and A to A, breaking the stitching at the front and back seams.
Trim all seam allowances to ¼ inch and snip all curves.
Turn the body right side out and stuff it firmly through the opening

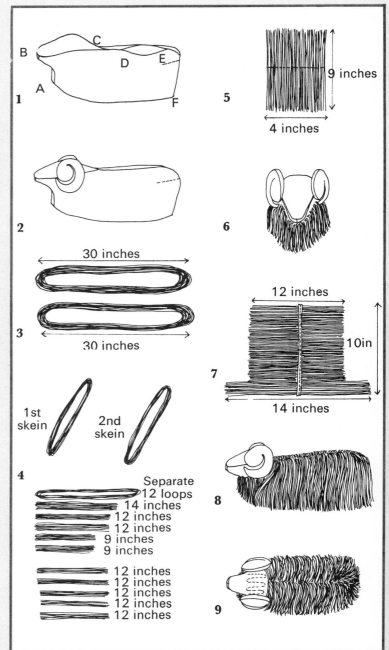

D to E. Close the opening with slip stitch (figure **1**).

The horns
Stitch the horns together in pairs, right sides facing, leaving an opening on each pair where marked. Trim the seam allowances to ¼ inch, trim across the corner G, and snip into the corner H and into the seam allowances on the curves.
Turn the horns right sides out and stuff them firmly, closing the openings with slip stitch. Attach firmly with slip stitch (figure **2**).

The woolen coat
Rewind the skeins of Aran yarn around two chairs so that the loops in each skein measure 60 inches (30 inches doubled) figure **3**. From the first skein separate 12 loops and wind this length of yarn over the 12 inch strip of paper to make a row of curls as shown for the large porcupine in Toymaking chapter 4, figure **3**, p. 892. Cut the rest of the first skein of yarn into two 9 inch bundles, one 14 inch bundle and two 12 inch bundles (discard the tiny

pieces of yarn left over), and cut the second skein of yarn into five 12 inch bundles (figure **4**).

The bib. Spread out the two 9 inch bundles of yarn and carefully machine stitch the centers of the strands together as shown in figure **5**. Firmly backstitch this to the body where marked so that it stretches from underneath each horn and across the front (figure **6**). Backstitch through the stitching on the yarn so that the two halves of the bib fold over neatly and hang down.

The coat. Spread out the other bundles of yarn and stitch them to the straight tape, through their centers, as shown in figure **7**. Stitch the 14 inch bundle on first and then the seven 12 inch bundles. Lay the coat across the back of the ram with the tape along the center back seam and the 14 inch lengths of yarn close to the horns so that they hang down and merge with the bib (figure **8**).

Sew the front edge of the tape to the head gusset to hold the coat in place.

Arrange the length of curls on the top of the head in a zigzag shape so that they just cover the front strands of the coat (the dotted lines in figure **9** show the placing for the curls). Sew the curls down firmly with backstitch.

Lift the coat from the back and fold it forward over the head. Cover the back and sides of the body with rubber cement and gently fold the coat back into position. Arrange the coat so that the body is evenly covered. Press the yarn strands into position, making sure that the coat and bib meet and there are no gaps. There is no need to sew the coat into place as the rubber cement will hold the tape and the underneath strands of yarn in position. Leave the cement to dry for 24 hours, pressing the coat down occasionally. Make the tail by gathering a few strands from the back of the coat and braiding them together.

Trim the lower edge of the coat and bib if necessary.

The eyes

Cut the outer eyes from white felt and the pupils from black felt, sew the pupils onto the eyes and then sew the completed eyes onto the head where marked, using small, neat stitches.

E

OPENING

DART

BO

C

Tracing patterns for Randy Ram

These patterns are without seam allowances. When cutting add ½ inch seam allowance to all pieces except eyes and pupils.

F

A

GRAIN OF FABRIC

BASE

CUT ONE

F

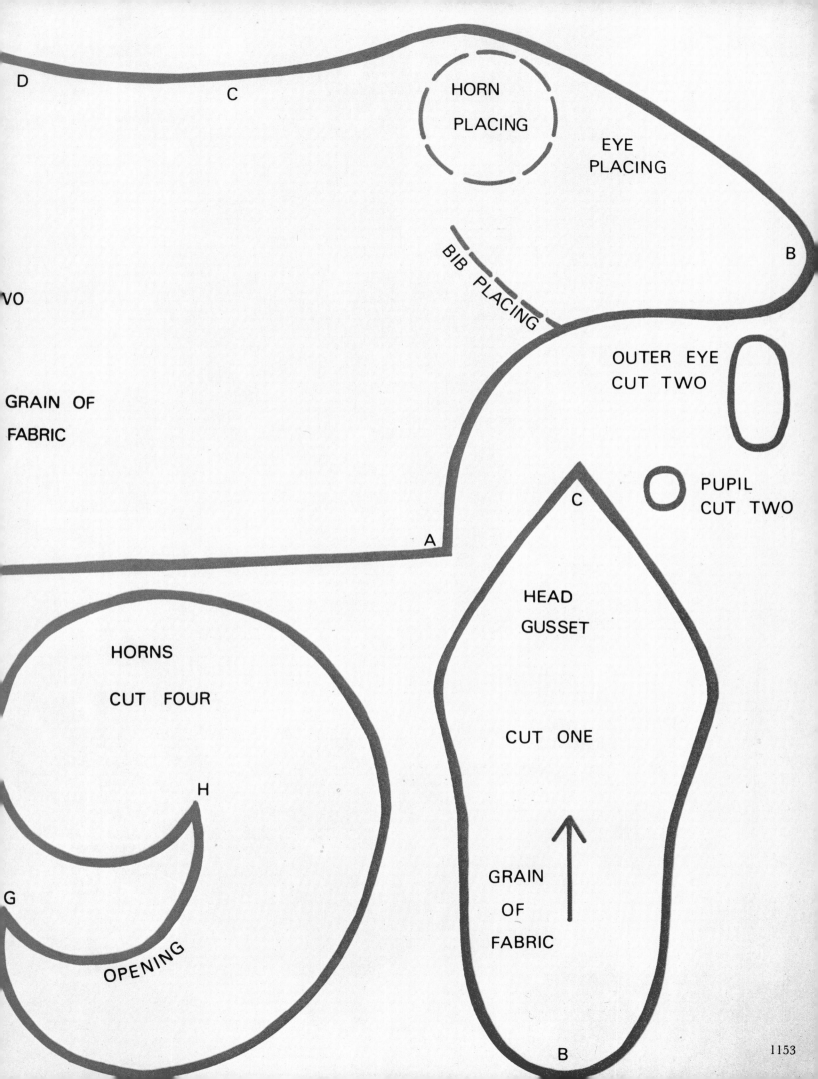

Collector's Piece

Embroidery for a dream

Romantic in concept and evocative of another age, the embroidered clothes illustrated on these pages were designed and made by Angela Salmon, a dress design student at London's St Martin's School of Art, for her final diploma exhibition. Although painstaking embroidery is not commercially viable in the ready-made clothing industry, it is comforting to know that students of design continue to produce exquisite work such as this, adapting traditional techniques to modern design concepts.

The lilac silk and black velvet dress, worn with pantaloons, has flowers and leaves of machine-embroidered organza applied to the bodice with realistic-looking plastic blackberries to complete the motif. The caped coat-dress, made of olive-colored chiffon, is worn over a strawberry printed chiffon dress. Strawberry flowers, leaves and fruit motifs, made of matte satin and machine-embroidered organza, are applied with some of the edges lying free of the background fabric.

The blue and white ensemble consists of a blue organza apron worn over a full-sleeved chiffon dress. The designer has chosen field flowers for her inspiration—poppies, buttercups, speedwell and wheat stalks—embroidered and applied to the background fabric. Surface embroidery has been added to enrich the design.

▼ *HRH Princess Anne, photographed for her 21st birthday in a dress made of a fabric designed by Susan Grist of St Martin's School*

The velvet touch

If you think that velvet is a difficult fabric to work with, your fears should be dispelled after reading this chapter. It gives a description of the various types of velvet you will use for dressmaking, followed by useful tips on how to choose suitable styles, and work and handle the fabric for really successful results.

Armed with this basic velvet know-how, there is no reason why you cannot feel as relaxed handling this most romantic fabric as any other. You might start with a glamorous long evening skirt and coordinate it with a silk, satin or crepe blouse for the exclusive look of the outfit featured opposite, from a Vogue Pattern. The chapter ends with special hints for making a velvet dress also using a Vogue Pattern, an obvious style choice since it lists velvet among the suitable fabrics to use. The instructions take you yet one step further in your dressmaking knowledge by telling you how to achieve a smooth finish for the beautiful contour seaming over the bust, a style feature of the pattern.

an alternative version
included in pattern

▲ *Back and front views of dress, Vogue Pattern*

Suitable fabrics and styles

Types of velvet
There are many types of velvet made from different fibers, as well as combinations of fibers, such as velvet with a cotton base and silk pile.

Their weight differs considerably too. Velvets are made as heavy as coating and as light as chiffon, and between these extremes are the easily worked dress velvets.

The most common and well known velvet is Lyons velvet, which is firm and usually made in pure silk. Rayon velvets are also common, they are made entirely from rayon and then treated for crease resist-

ance. Both Lyons and rayon velvet have short pile which makes them ideal for the beginner.

Panne velvets are also good for the beginner but are not always available as they are dependent on prevailing fashion. The nap or pile of panne velvet is brushed flat and in one direction. These velvets are often printed and the pile gives depth and texture to a printed design.

French street or coat velvets are quite light in weight, but the pile is somewhat deep and it becomes a little more difficult to work. Recently a velvet has appeared which is washable. This has a most luxurious surface but can be treated almost like an ordinary flat weave. This velvet is made from a man-made fiber, the appearance of which resembles ordinary artificial silk. Not only does it wash easily and wear well, but it is also quite inexpensive.

Since this velvet is suitable for washing it is the obvious choice for garments in light colors.

Cotton velveteen is a different type of fabric. Here the base and pile are both made of cotton. Velveteen is made to resemble velvet but the construction of the weave is different. There is really no problem in making a garment from this fabric.

Choosing the velvet
As the textures of velvet vary, consider the fit and hang you require for the style of garment and choose the velvet accordingly. If you are a beginner use a short nap velvet to get used to working on velvets before attempting the longer pile ones. So look for a good close pile which feels firm in the hand and will allow you to work with the fabric without too much slipping.

Choosing a suitable design
Avoid styles which rely on heavy darting for the fit as darts are difficult to press in velvet.

The beginner should also avoid styles which are cut in one with no dividing waist seam. It is best to learn to sew velvet on smaller sections of a garment as the seams are easier to control.

The Vogue Pattern featured in this chapter incorporates all the above qualities and is therefore a particularly suitable design for working with velvet.

General hints

Supporting fabrics
Interfacing. It is rare for velvet garments to need interfacing, especially when there is a loose lining attached to the neck and armhole lines.

Facings. Facings must be kept to a minimum to avoid heavy rolls on the edges of the garment. It is best to face velvet garments with matching silk bias facings which are neat and firm.

Interlinings. Few velvets benefit from inter or underlinings and the stitching of seams in underlined velvet can become a nightmare, since the whole seam appears to move.

To support full skirts in velvet, always construct a suitable under garment and do not use stiff linings or underlinings. Stiff fabrics will catch the pile on the inside of the fabric and slowly drag it out, resulting in bald patches all over the surface.

Hand-sewing
Hand-sewing should be practiced on a scrap of velvet. If the stitches are made too timidly they only catch the loops of the pile where it is anchored into the weave and gradually pull it out. So make sure you catch the weave but don't allow the stitches to mark the pile.

Background: Evening dress from a Vogue Pattern in rayon velvet
Foreground: Velvet skirt with crepe blouse also from a Vogue Pattern

Seam finishes

Seam finishes in velvet garments should be done by hand as a machine finish can cause a seam edge to tighten and roll, making it appear wrinkled on the outside. Do not be tempted to use pinking shears as this will only encourage fraying.

Zipper fasteners

It is often mistakenly thought that you require a fine zipper to fasten a velvet dress. Fine zippers usually come with a fine tape, and as you stitch the fine tape to the seamline through the folded thickness of the fabric, it is pulled with the stitches into the depth of the pile and there is no control or anchorage to hold the stitches in position. It does not matter how much you try, your zipper will always look wrinkled.

So always use a strong dress zipper with a cotton tape. This is slightly stiff and firm and will allow you to sew it in position without its puckering.

Tools for ironing velvet

For ironing velvet you should use a needleboard.

Needleboards are squares of wire pile anchored to a firm base. The fabric is then pressed with pile down on the needleboard. It is worthwhile buying an expensive one as a cheap needleboard can ruin the velvet.

You can of course draw your seams over an ordinary iron standing on its end and covered with a damp cloth. To do this, open the seam allowance and draw the seam section by section over the iron, patting the velvet gently on the outside with a soft brush.

Needleboards are obtainable in the notions departments of some stores. But if you cannot find what you are looking for, try one of the special stores selling dressmaker's equipment. They will also stock very narrow strips of needleboard which you lay over a sleeveboard to press the seams in fitted sleeves.

Stitching velvet

When stitching velvet the pressure of the upper presser foot on most sewing machines needs to be reduced unless the machine is self-adjusting. To test for this, place two scraps of velvet face to face and make a row of basting stitches as for a seamline. Stitch along the seamline. If the seam begins to twist, loosen the pressure and stitch again. Repeat until the fabric stops twisting and the seam remains flat.

For stitching velvet use a fine soft thread such as pure silk sewing thread. Carefully adjust the stitch tension on the machine, since the fabric is thick and a tightly set stitch tension will cause it to pucker.

Making a velvet dress

The pattern

The Vogue Pattern used has a high waistline and is semi-fitted. The shaping is achieved by contour seams over the bust, which are continued with corresponding seams in the skirt. The front seams of the skirt have soft unpressed pleats.

Checking the pattern for proportion

High waist seams, like low waist seams, need careful proportioning and must therefore be adjusted to suit your height. This is easily done by comparing the following measurements. First pin the pattern together, joining skirt and bodice. On the skirt pattern you will find the indication for the natural waistline. Use this mark to check your own waist length and that of the pattern. Make any necessary adjustments on the given shortening or lengthening lines.

Then check that the height of the waist seam is right for you. Measure the distance from the center of your shoulder to the bust and from bust to waist.

If your bustline is approximately half or not more than two thirds of the distance between shoulder and waist, you can safely use the given proportion on the pattern. If the bustline is lower than two thirds of the distance between shoulder and waist and you are slim, lower the high waistline a little to avoid making you look short waisted. Mark the bodice pattern section for extra seam allowance at the waist, so that you can make final adjustments when fitting.

Large sizes who have the problem of a low bustline should not use this pattern. Next compare the positions of the large 0 symbols on the pattern with your bustline.

You will find ease built into the pattern between the large 0 symbols on the Front pattern, to allow the seam to fit smoothly over the bust when the sections are stitched together.

Check that this part of the pattern is the same height as your own bustline. If not, make the necessary adjustment now by moving the position of the symbols either up or down, up to $\frac{1}{2}$ inch only, on both Front pattern pieces (figure **1**).

Select the sleeve length and neckline you want to make and adjust the pattern skirt length to your requirements.

If you follow Creative Hands instructions you will not need the facing patterns. After all the above adjustments have been made you are ready to cut out.

Layout and finding direction of pile

Before cutting velvet decide which way you want the pile to run. For a full glowing effect cut it so that the pile runs upward. But for garments which will have more than occasional wear, it is best to have the pile running down, especially in darker colors which are already full of bloom in either direction. A pile running upward is inclined to retain particles of dust which eventually show up in those places of the garment which are subject to wear.

Some velvets show the pile direction quite clearly—as you look into the pile from the selvage, you will see a distinct tilt of the fibers. But with many velvets today it is difficult to detect the direction of the pile, so make the following test. Hang both ends of the fabric length up side by side. The shiny side is the pile running down and the dull side is the pile running up. To avoid confusion later, chalk an arrow in the direction of the pile on the back of the fabric.

Use the cutting instructions on the layout sheet in the pattern envelope.

When you arrange velvet for a folded layout, make sure you have the pile facing out, as a pile laid face to face can result in the layers sticking together, causing you to cut uneven sections of the garment.

Marking the pattern detail

Basting and marking velvet must be done with great care, and a fine soft thread such as pure silk sewing thread should be used. Do not use too many tailor's tacks and mark the most essential places and symbols of the pattern only. Basting stitches can get caught up in the pile and when removed they drag out the fibers.

If you must tailor's tack a seamline, always work outside the actual stitching line.

Preparing for fitting

Pin and baste the garment together ready for fitting, using the steps shown to assemble the dress on the instruction sheet. If you want to use the stay-stitching method shown in the instructions, try it on a scrap of velvet first to make sure that it does not mark the fabric.

Stay-stitching is not necessary on firmly backed fabrics and is only a precaution. After basting do not press the seams open as for sheer fabrics.

Fitting

Slip on the basted dress and pin the Center Back opening.

The dress should hang close to the body but without fitting into the waist contours. The fitting over the bust may need some adjustment, so use the contour seams but do not remove all the ease by pinning the seams too close into the figure between bustline and armholes. This would shorten the side front section and distort the armhole size.

Make sure that the depth of the front pleats in the skirt is anchored firmly in the waist seam and that the pleats do not fall away toward the hemline.

Check the waist fitting, the length, and the neck and armhole lines.

Making the dress

Mark the fitting corrections carefully and correct any uneven pin lines. Transfer the corrections to the paper pattern to cut the loose lining.

Separate bodice and skirt and make each section before joining them.

The bodice. Rip the shoulder seams and stitch the contour and side seams.

Snip the seam allowance on the contour seams where it strains when opened for pressing, then press. To do this, place the section to be pressed on the needleboard, pile down, hold the seam allowance open and gently place the iron on it. Do not press down hard, but lift the iron and replace it until the seam allowance remains flat. Work into the bustline starting at the lower edge of the bodice toward the fullest part. Then turn the bodice around and work from the armhole edge.

Always keep to the seam allowance; do not put the iron on the surrounding fabric as this will cause it to mark.

Press the side seams open.

Stitch the back shoulder darts, slash the darts along the center fold and press open. Stitch and press the shoulder seams, and overcast all the seam allowances.

If you are making a loose lining, make the lining bodice the same as the dress bodice and join dress and lining neckline and armhole seams with firm basting stitches in a matching thread. This is necessary since basting stitches in these seams can easily get caught up in the machine stitches and become difficult to remove.

The neckline. If the dress is made without a collar, finish the neckline as follows.

Prepare a bias facing from the lining fabric curving it to the shape of the neckline (see Dressmaking chapter 11, page 216). Before you attach the facing, cut a stay tape from the lining fabric selvage, $\frac{3}{8}$ inch wide, and pin and baste to the neck seam with the center of the stay tape over the stitching line (figure **2**).

Make the basting stitches just inside the seam allowance to avoid catching them in the machine stitches. Then pin and baste the shaped facing to the neckline, easing it slightly into the steep curves. Stitch the facing to the dress and trim the seam allowance on the dress neckline. Snip the seam allowance on the dress but

not on the bias facing.

Pin and edge-baste the facing to the inside of the garment, rolling it under as shown in Dressmaking chapter 11, page 216. This will stop the movement of the velvet dragging the seamline to the edge.

Hand sew the seam allowance of the facing to the lining. Then fold under the raw edge of the facing and sew it to the lining with invisible hemming stitches. Leave the ends of the facing loose to insert the zipper.

The skirt. Stitch the seams with the bias of the fabric to avoid adverse action of the face to face pile (see Dressmaking chapter 27, page 536).

If you find you cannot control the movement of the fabric, make a second row of basting stitches outside the seamline to give the seam more support when stitching. Press the seams as for the bodice and press that part of each pleat which has been stitched together.

Overcast the seam edges and make the lining skirt without pleats (figure **3**). Finish off the seam allowance on the lining and join lining skirt to lining bodice. Join the dress skirt to the dress bodice and press the waist seams open.

Inserting the zipper. Cut the lining from the neckline seam at the Center Back, to allow the seam allowance to be folded back freely (figure **4**). Press back the dress seam allowance of the Center Back opening carefully and hand sew the zipper in using a prick stitch. Fold the lining over the edge of the zipper tape in the usual way and hand sew in place.

Fold in the seam allowances on the facing and hand sew over the ends of the zipper tape. Fasten the top of the opening with a hand-worked bar and a hook (figure **5**).

Finishing. Pin and then hand sew the seam allowances of the waist seam on the lining and the dress together with short running stitches. Try on the dress and make a final check for length.

The hem. Hems in velvet dresses cannot be let down, so you must be sure that you have the right length.

As with all curved hems, do not leave more than a· $1\frac{1}{2}$ inch hem allowance, otherwise the bulk will keep the hem from remaining flat.

Ease in the fullness around the top edge of the hem allowance, make neat and then hand sew in position using an invisible hemming stitch.

To finish the inside of the pleats at the hem edge follow the appropriate step on the pattern instruction sheet.

Remove all the basting stitches before pressing and do not press the hem of the dress too hard.

Make the lining hem about 1 inch shorter than the dress hem.

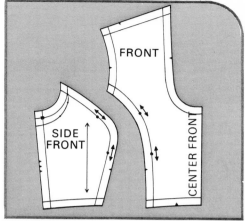

▲ **1.** *Adjusting the ease over the bustline*

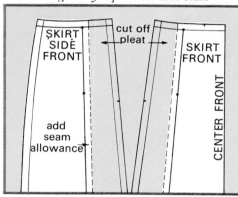

▲ **2.** *Basting a stay tape to the neck seam*

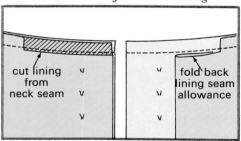

▲ **3.** *Pattern alteration for the skirt lining*

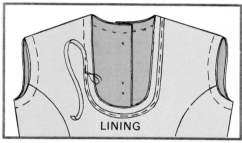

▲ **4.** *Lining cut from neck, shown without facing*
▼ **5.** *The finished back opening*

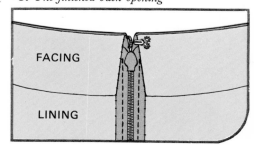

Hearts and flowers

This hearts and flowers design traced straight from the page would look charming worked in chain stitch outlines and fillings. Alternatively, it could be worked simply in backstitch. Enlarged, it could be used as a design for appliqué. The design is particularly suitable for decorating tablecloths, and the central heart motif can be worked on the corner of table napkins to match.

Pattern Library

Frosted pine

Chain stitch is ideal for embroidering curved or twisted lines. Here it has been used to depict the pine needles on a branch. The cones are worked in solid areas of satin stitch surrounded with chain stitch, and it is interesting to notice the realistic treatment of the cones in contrast to the freer treatment of the pine needles.

White six-strand floss has given the embroidery the crisp sparkling look of frosted pine trees in winter, and the design lends itself well to linen for Christmas.

Glitter knitting with beads and sequins

It is best to add beads or sequins to knitting while the fabric is being worked.

Choice of beads and sequins

Care when choosing beads and sequins for knitting will pay in the results obtained. Because large, heavy beads will drag the knitting out of shape, small beads are usually a better choice. If the beads are to be worked close together they should only cover a small area, because even with small beads a large area would soon become too heavy for the yarn.

It is always better to make sure that beads or sequins will not lose their color, and only those guaranteed suitable for dry cleaning are advisable. All beaded and sequined garments should be dry-cleaned, with the exception of those with small, lightweight plastic beads, which are usually washable.

Choice of stitch

Beads or sequins are decorative enough in themselves and should only be combined with fancy stitches if these genuinely contribute to the finished apperance.

Because of its smooth surface, stockinette stitch forms the most suitable background to show the decoration to best advantage.

Threading beads or sequins onto yarn

Occasionally it is possible to buy lightweight beads or sequins with large holes, in which case there is no problem threading them onto the yarn. However, the usual bead or sequin used for knitting has a

▼ *Placing a bead on a knit row*

▼ *Purling stitch after placing bead*

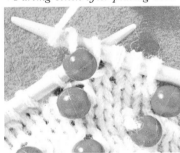

▼ *Placing a bead on a purl row*

▼ *Knitting stitch following bead*

relatively small hole which is not large enough to take a needle threaded with yarn.

In such a case, cut a length of sewing thread about 8 inches long and thread both ends into the eye of the needle. Slide the needle halfway along the doubled thread, thus forming a loop at one end. Smooth both the ends and the loop downward. Pass the end of the yarn into the loop for several inches and then smooth the double thickness of the yarn downward.

Slip the beads or sequins onto the needle, over the sewing thread and then the yarn.

Adding beads between stitches on a purl row

Purl along the row to the bead position, take the yarn behind the needle, slip a bead along next to the needle, knit the next stitch and return the yarn ready for purling.

Continue in purl until the next bead position. Work the next bead in exactly the same way.

Adding beads between stitches on a knit row

Work to the point where the bead is to be placed. Bring the yarn forward toward you and slip a bead up close to the needle, purl the next stitch, then continue knitting in the normal way until the next bead position is reached.

Adding beads (or sequins) in front of a stitch on a knit row

Knit to the desired position, bring the yarn forward and slip a bead close up to the fabric, slip the next stitch from the left-hand needle without knitting it and leaving the bead in front of the slipped stitch. Return the yarn to the knitting position and work to the next bead position.

Adding beads (or sequins) in front of a stitch on a purl row

Purl to the bead position. Take the yarn back to right side of work and slip bead up to the needle, slip next stitch, carry yarn across slipped stitch on

right side, bring yarn back and purl to next bead position.

Alternative method of adding sequins

The type of sequin which has a hole close to the edge must be able to hang. With either of the previous methods, the sequins would be distorted. Instead, use either of the following methods after threading the sequins onto the yarn.

Working a knit row. Knit to the point where the sequin is to be placed, knit the next stitch through the back of the loop, pushing the sequin through the actual stitch from back to front.

Working a purl row. Work to the point where the sequin is to be placed, push the sequin close to the needle, purl the next stitch. This stitch holds the sequin in place without having to push it through. Once the sequin is in place, continue along the row as usual on a purl row to the next sequin position.

Evening bag

Size

Top edge, approx 5in.
Depth including fringe, 7in.

> **Gauge**
> 8 sts and 12 rows to 1in worked on No.3 needles.

Materials

Unger's Cruise
1-4/10oz. ball
One pair No.3 needles
(or Canadian No.10)
624 small pearl beads
One handbag frame
¼yd lining material

To work the bag

Thread beads onto ball of yarn.
Using No.3 needles, cast on 39 sts.
1st row K.
2nd and every other row K1, P to last st, K1.
3rd row K4, *ytf, slip bead close to work, slip next st keeping bead in front, ytb— called B1—, K5, rep from * to last 5 sts, B1, K4.

▼ Threading beads onto the yarn   *▲ Glitter yarn enhanced by pearl beads adds glamour to an evening bag*

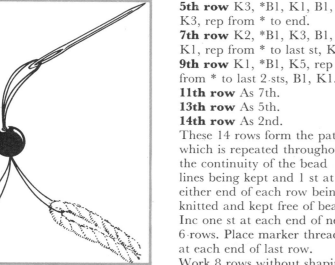

5th row K3, *B1, K1, B1, K3, rep from * to end.
7th row K2, *B1, K3, B1, K1, rep from * to last st, K1.
9th row K1, *B1, K5, rep from * to last 2 sts, B1, K1.
11th row As 7th.
13th row As 5th.
14th row As 2nd.
These 14 rows form the patt which is repeated throughout, the continuity of the bead lines being kept and 1 st at either end of each row being knitted and kept free of beads. Inc one st at each end of next 6 rows. Place marker thread at each end of last row.
Work 8 rows without shaping.

Dec 1 st at each end of next and every 4th row until 41 sts remain, every other row until 33 sts remain, then every row until 21 sts remain. Bind off 3 sts at beg of next 4 rows. Bind off.

Fringe
With RS facing, pick up and K72 sts between marker threads around the lower half of the bag (i.e. along one side, across bound-off sts and along other side).
Loop row *Insert needle into next st on left-hand needle, wind yarn over needle point and around 3 fingers of left

hand 3 times, then around needle point once, draw loops through and return to left-hand needle, K into back of loops and st (see Knitting Know-how 58, p. 1142), rep from * to end of row. Bind off. Work a second side in the same manner, omitting fringe.

Finishing
Cut lining slightly larger than knitted section.
Place 2 sections of knitting right sides together and join along bound-off edge of fringe. Seam lining along same edges. Stitch bag to frame. Insert lining and slip stitch in place.

Knitted jacket full of zip

A zippered casual jacket designed to fit all sizes from teens to adults.

Sizes

Directions are for 32in bust or chest.

The figures in brackets [] refer to the 34, 36, 38, 40 and 42in sizes respectively.

Length from shoulder, 22[22:23½:23½:25:25]in, adjustable.

Sleeve seam, 17[17½:17½: 18:18:18]in, adjustable.

Gauge

12 sts and 15 rows to 2in over patt worked on No.5 needles

Materials

Reynolds Tweed
Courtelle 40gm balls
9[9:10:10:11:12] balls
One pair No.4 knitting needles (or Canadian No.9)
One pair No.5 knitting needles (or Canadian No.8)
One 20[20:22:22:24:24]in open-ended zipper

Back

Using No.4 needles, cast on 99 [105:111:117:123:129] sts.

1st row Sl 1, *K1, P1, rep from * to last 2 sts, K2.

2nd row Sl 1, *P1, K1, rep from * to end.

Rep these 2 rows 5 times more. Change to No.5 needles. Commence patt.

1st row Sl 1, K0[1:0:1:0:1], *P2, K2, rep from * to last 2[3:2:3:2:3] sts, P1[2:1:2:1:2], K1.

2nd row Sl 1, P0[1:0:1:0:1], *K2, P2, rep from * to last 2[3:2:3:2:3] sts, K2[3:2:3:2:3].

1164

These 2 rows form patt and are rep throughout.

Continue in patt until work measures 14½[14½:15:15: 15½:15½]in from beg, or desired length to underarm, ending with a WS row.

Shape raglan sleeves

Bind off 4 sts at beg of next 2 rows.

Keeping patt correct, dec one st at each end of every row until 61[55:69:63:77:71] sts rem, then every other row until 27[27:29:29:31:31] sts rem.

Bind off.

Right front

Using No.4 needles, cast on 49[51:55:57:61:63] sts.

Work 12 rows rib as given for Back, inc one st at beg of last row for the 34 and 42in sizes

▼ *Stitch detail showing zipper*

only. 49[52:55:57:61:64] sts. Change to No.5 needles. Commence patt.

32 and 40in sizes only

1st row Sl 1, *K2, P2, rep from * to last 4 sts, K2, P1, K1.

2nd row As 1st.

34 and 42in sizes only

1st row Sl 1, *P2, K2, rep from * to last 3 sts, P2, K1.

2nd row Sl 1, P1, *K2, P2, rep from * to last 2 sts, K2.

36 and 38in sizes only

Work 2 rows patt as given for Back.

All sizes

Continue in patt until work measures same as Back to raglan shaping, ending with a RS row.

Shape raglan sleeves

Bind off 4 sts at beg of next row.

Keeping patt correct, dec one st at raglan edge on every row until 30[27:34:30:38:35] sts rem, then on every other row until work measures 19[19:21:21:23:23]in from beg, ending with a WS row.

Shape neck

Next row At neck edge bind off 5[5:6:5:7:7] sts, patt to last 2 sts, K2 tog.

Continue dec at raglan edge as before, *at the same time* dec one st at neck edge on next 6 rows.

Continue shaping raglan edge only until 2 sts rem. Bind off.

Left front

Using No.4 needles, cast on 49[51:55:57:61:63] sts.

Work 12 rows rib as given for Back, inc one st at end of last row for the 34 and 42in sizes only. 49[52:55:57:61:64] sts.

Change to No.5 needles. Commence patt.

32 and 40in sizes only

1st row Sl 1, P1, *K2, P2, rep from * to last 3 sts, K3.

2nd row As 1st.

34 and 42in size only

1st row Sl 1, *P2, K2, rep from * to last 3 sts, P2, K1.

2nd row Sl 1, K1, *P2, K2, rep from * to last 2 sts, K2.

36 and 38in sizes only

Work 2 patt rows as given for Back.

All sizes

Keeping patt correct and reversing all shaping, complete to correspond to Right front.

Sleeves

Using No.4 needles, cast on 43[45:47:49:51:53] sts.

Work 13 rows in rib as given for Back.

Next row Rib 4[1:2:3:4:1], *inc in next st, rib 4[5:5:5:5:6], rep from * to last 4[2:3:4:5:3] sts, inc in next st, rib to end. 51[53:55:57:59:61] sts.

Change to No.5 needles and patt as given for Back, inc one st at each end of 3rd and every following 7th row until there are 83[85:87:89:91:93] sts, working extra sts into patt.

Continue without shaping until sleeve measures 17[17½:17½:18:18:18]in from beg, or desired length to underarm. End with a WS row.

Shape raglan sleeves

Bind off 4 sts at beg of next 2 rows.

Keeping patt correct, dec one st at each end of every row until 53[51:65:63:77:75] sts rem, then every other row until 15 sts rem. Bind off.

Neckband

Join raglan seams.

Using No.4 needles, with RS work facing pick up and K 17[17:18:18:19:19] sts from right front neck edge, 15 sts from sleeve, 27[27:29: 29:31:31] sts from back neck, 15 sts from sleeve and 17[17: 18:18:19:19] sts from left front neck edge. 91[91:95:95:99:99] sts.

Beg with the 2nd row, work 2in rib as given for Back. Bind off loosely in rib.

Finishing

Press lightly with a cool iron under a dry cloth on the WS. Join side and sleeve seams. Sew in sleeves. Fold neckband in half and sl st to WS. Sew in zipper. Press seams.

His and hers zippered jacket ►

Beads and sequins in crochet

Crochet Know-how 59

This chapter tells you how to crochet beads or sequins directly into a piece of work.

Beads or sequins worked into crochet are an attractive way of giving additional interest and color.

Choice of beads and sequins
The choice of beads will depend on the thickness of the yarn to be used. Never choose large, heavy beads for a fine yarn because they will pull it out of shape. The finer or softer the yarn, the smaller the beads need to be. If the beads are to decorate a garment, make sure that they are suitable for dry cleaning.

Because they are so light, most sequins are suitable, provided they can be dry cleaned.

Threading beads or sequins
Where a bead or sequin with a large hole is to be used, it is possible to thread directly onto the yarn with a needle before working.

Most beads and sequins, however, have a small hole through which the bulk of the yarn and needle eye would not pass. In this case, cut a piece of sewing thread 8in long and thread both ends into the eye of the needle. Slide the needle halfway along the doubled thread, thus forming a loop at one end. Smooth both the ends and the loop downward. Pass the end of the yarn into the loop for several inches and then smooth the double thickness of the yarn downward.

Thread the beads or sequins onto the needle, over the sewing thread and then the yarn.

1166

Single crochet
Although the beads lie on the right side of the fabric, they may be worked in on either a right side or a wrong side row. It is possible to leave several stitches between beads and several plain rows between bead rows.

Adding on a wrong side row. Begin a wrong side row in the usual way, working along to the bead position. Insert hook into next stitch, yrh and draw through loop, slip bead up close against the right side of the work, yrh taking the yarn from just beyond the bead and draw through both loops.

Adding on a right side row. Work to the first bead position. Insert the hook into the next stitch from back to front, slip bead up close to hook, yrh from beyond bead and draw the loop through to the back of the work, yrh and draw through all sts. Continue along the row.

Double crochet
Adding on a right side row. Work to the first bead position, yrh, slip bead up close to the, hook, insert hook into next st, yrh and draw through loops, yrh and draw through two loops, yrh and draw through remaining loops.

Adding on a wrong side row. The bead is added just before the last stage of the dc. Work in dc to bead position, yrh, insert hook into next st, and draw loop through, yrh and draw through two loops, slip bead up close to fabric on RS, yrh taking yarn from beyond bead and draw through remaining loops.

▲ *Slipping bead close to fabric on a wrong side single crochet row*

▲ *Completing the single crochet stitch after placing bead on wrong side row*

▲ *Putting yarn around hook from beyond bead on right side single crochet row*

Choker

Size
Width of choker, 1in
Length of choker, 12in, adjustable

Gauge
Center motif measures $1\frac{5}{8}$in

Materials
J. & P. Coats Six Cord Mercerized No.20
1 ball One No. B (2.00 mm) crochet hook
Two hooks and eyes for fastening
28 pearl beads (if length is altered, fewer or more beads will be required)

Center motif
Thread 8 beads onto yarn.
1st round Wind yarn 10 times around tip of finger, remove from finger and work 32sc into ring, join with ss into first sc.
2nd round 1sc into same place as ss, *ch5, skip 3sc, 1sc into next sc, rep from * skipping 1sc at end of last rep, join with ss into first sc.
3rd round 2sc into first ch loop, insert hook into same ch loop, slip bead up to hook, yrh from beyond bead and, draw loop through ch letting bead come to front of work, yrh and draw through both loops—called 1 bead sc—, ch3, 5dc into bead sc worked before ch3, ch2, 1 ss into same sc—called 1 shell—, 2sc into

▲ *Yarn around hook for first stage of double crochet on right side row*

▲ *Double crochet wrong side row*

▲ *Completing double crochet*

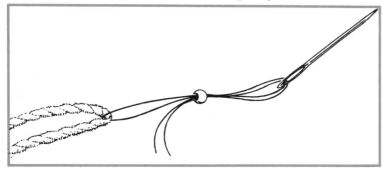

▲ *Method for threading beads or sequins onto yarn*

▲ *A pretty beaded choker which is simple to make in crochet cotton*

same ch loop, *into next ch loop work 2sc, 1 bead sc, 1 shell and 2sc, rep from * ending with ss into first sc. Fasten off.

First side of neckband

Thread 10 beads onto yarn or additional beads if length is more than 12in.

1st row Commence with *ch3, 1dc into 3rd ch from hook—called 1 ring—, rep from * 19 times more or until work measures ½in more than desired length from outer edge of Center motif to center back of neck, having an even number of rings. Do not turn.

2nd row *Into next ring work 1sc, ch2, 1sc*, rep from * to * to within last ring, into next ring work 1sc, ch2, 3sc into

end of ring, ch2 and 1sc into other side, working into opposite side of rings rep from * to * to within opposite side of last ring, into last ring work 1sc, ch2 and 2sc, join with ss into first sc.

3rd row Ss into first ch loop, 1sc into same ch loop, *ch5, 1sc into next ch loop, ch3, 1sc into next ch loop, rep from * to within 3sc at end of neckband, skipping 1sc at end of last rep, skip 1sc, 1sc into next sc, **ch3, 1sc into next ch loop, rep from ** ending with ch3, skip 1sc, 1sc into next dc, ch3, join with ss into first sc.

4th row *Into next ch loop work 2sc, 1 bead sc, 1 shell and 2sc, 3sc into next ch loop, rep from * to within sc

at end of neckband, 3sc into next ch loop, 1ss into next sc, ch3, 3dc into each ch loop to within last 2 loops, ch2, 1ss into next sc, 3sc into each of next ch2 loops, join with ss into first sc. Turn.

5th row Ch1, 1sc into each of next 6sc, 3sc over next ch2 loop, 1sc into each dc, 3sc over next ch3 loop, 1sc into each of next 6sc. Turn.

6th row Ch1, 1sc into first sc, ch1, 1ss into center dc of any shell on center motif, ch1, 1ss into last sc on neckband, 1sc into each of next 7sc, ch1, 1ss into center dc of next shell on center motif, ch1, 1ss into last sc on neckband, 3sc into next sc, 1sc into each sc to within last 9sc, 3sc into next sc, 1sc into each sc to end.

Second side of neckband

Work first 5 rows as given for first side of neckband.

6th row 1sc into each of first 8sc, 3sc into next sc, 1sc into each sc to within last 9sc, 3sc into next sc, 1sc into next sc, ch1, skip 2 shells at top of center motif, 1ss into center dc of next shell, ch1, 1ss into last sc on neckband, 1sc into each of next 6sc, ch1, 1ss into center dc of next shell on center motif, ch1, 1ss into last sc on neckband, 1sc into next sc. Fasten off.

Finishing

Press under a damp cloth with a warm iron on a felt or foam pad to protect beads.
Sew hooks and eyes to ends of neckband to fasten.

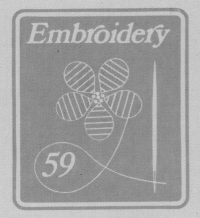

Butterflies and summer flowers

1

4

These delightful butterfly motifs, worked in cross-stitch on a medium weave fabric, are typical of the freshness associated with Scandinavian table linen designs. Worked to the size of the charts on pages 1170 and 1171, the motifs will make table mats measuring about 6 inches square. Worked on coarser weaves, so that the motifs are enlarged, the butterflies can be used for a square tablecloth, worked in the corners or in the center. A single motif would also make a charming pillow design or, mounted in a small frame, a pretty picture.

To make the set of six mats, each measuring 6 inches by 6 inches, you will need:
- ☐ ⅓ yd 60 inch wide ecru colored linen with 25 threads to 1 inch.
- ☐ Tapestry needle No.24
- ☐ D.M.C. 6-strand floss in the following colors and amounts:
    One skein each of—
    brown 975, light orange 973, medium orange 972, light mauve 210, dark pink 600, light mustard 834, dark mustard 832, dark orange 971, dark mauve 552, light blue 996, dark blue 995.
    Two skeins each of—
    dark green 470, light green 471

Use D.M.C. 6-strand floss in the following colors for each mat
Mat No. 1—975, 973, 972, 210, 600, 470, 834, 832.
Mat No. 2—975, 971, 972, 973, 471, 470, 834, 832.
Mat No. 3—210, 552, 996, 995, 471, 470, 834, 832.
Mat No. 4—600, 996, 995, 972, 971, 470, 834, 832, 471.
Mat No. 5—975, 604, 602, 600, 210, 552, 470, 834, 832.
Mat No. 6—975, 973, 972, 971, 604, 602, 600, 471, 470, 834, 832.

Working the mats

For each mat, cut a square of fabric measuring 10 inches by 10 inches on the straight grain of the fabric. Prepare the work by drawing out two threads on all four sides, 2¼ inches from the edge. Overcast the edges to prevent fraying. Refer to the photographs as a guide to the placing of each design and work, following the graphs. Work cross-stitches over two threads of fabric each way using two strands of floss in the needle. The solid areas are worked in cross-stitch and the single lines, such as those for the butterflies' antennae and legs, in double running stitch.

Making the mats

When the embroidery is completed, press on the wrong side over a damp cloth. Cut away the surplus fabric to within 1¼ inches from drawn threads on each edge. Make a hem all around each mat ¼ inch deep, miter the corners and turn up the hem to the very edge of the drawn threads and baste. Secure the hem with handkerchief hem stitch (see Embroidery chapter 21, page 414), picking up two drawn threads at a time and pulling the working thread firmly to bunch each group.

2

3

5

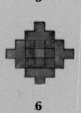

6

3

6

Chevron stitches and making a doorstop

Here are four more textured stitches for covering large areas of canvas or for working interesting textured backgrounds to designs. Work them in grouped areas of strongly contrasting colors for the brilliant effects shown on the doorstop.

Rep stitch

A stitch worked in vertical rows on double-weave canvas.

Worked in a thick yarn which completely covers the canvas, the stitch resembles the fabric from which it takes its name.

Basket filling stitch

This is a surface filling stitch usually worked on counted threads, but it makes an ideal

needlepoint stitch, giving a lovely texture for a background. Interesting effects can be achieved by using two tones of one color.

Fishbone stitch

This stitch is worked over three horizontal and three vertical threads of double-thread canvas. Each long stitch is caught down with a short stitch across one double thread of canvas. It is worked in alternate rows from top to bottom and from the bottom upward. The stitch makes a good grounding stitch and can be equally successful when worked on single-weave canvas.

Knitting stitch

This stitch resembles chain stitch but it is worked in a similar way to stem stitch in

vertical rows. It is used only on double-thread canvas. Bring the needle out at the top and insert it two holes down and across to the left. Bring the needle out two holes across and one hole up to the right and continue to the end of the row. The second row is worked in reverse from bottom to top.

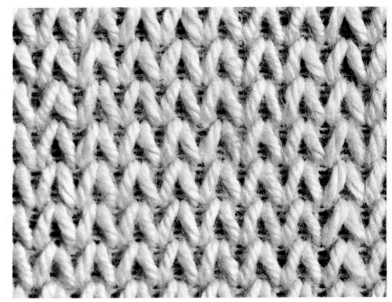

▲ *Knitting stitch worked on double-thread canvas*

▲ *Fishbone stitch in a single color*   ▼ *Fishbone stitch in four colors*

To make a brick doorstop you will need

- □ ½yd of double- or single-weave canvas about 24 inches wide
- □ A small piece of burlap or felt for backing
- □ One brick
- □ Yarns
- □ Tapestry needle and a crewel needle for sewing up

Making the pattern

Lay the brick on a sheet of paper and draw all around the base. Tip the brick onto a long side, keeping the edge exactly along the longest edge of the line already drawn, and draw around this side. Tip the brick onto a short end and draw again. A pattern will result shaped like the diagram. Cut the shape out. Baste the shape to the canvas, making sure that the edges run exactly in line with the thread of the canvas, and outline it with a felt-tipped pen. Remove the paper pattern and mark the center of the pattern with two lines of basting. Also mark the edges of the top area of the brick so that you can plan the design centrally.

Work the pattern shape with a stitched design. Block and trim away the excess canvas allowing ⅝ inch turnings of raw canvas (see Needlepoint, 5, p. 112). Slash into the corners to within ¼ inch of the stitching and cut across the outer corners diagonally to within ¼ inch of the point of stitching. Fold all the seam allowances to the back of the work, miter the corners and baste. With the right side of the work facing you, bring A and B together and seam, using the seam method given in Needlepoint chapter 5. Seam the remaining three corners in the same way. Now cut a piece of burlap or felt for the base of the brick (if using felt, no turnings are required). Fold turnings to the wrong side of fabric, baste and press carefully.

Slip the needlepoint over the brick, pin the piece of burlap or felt to the base and overcast it firmly to the canvas.

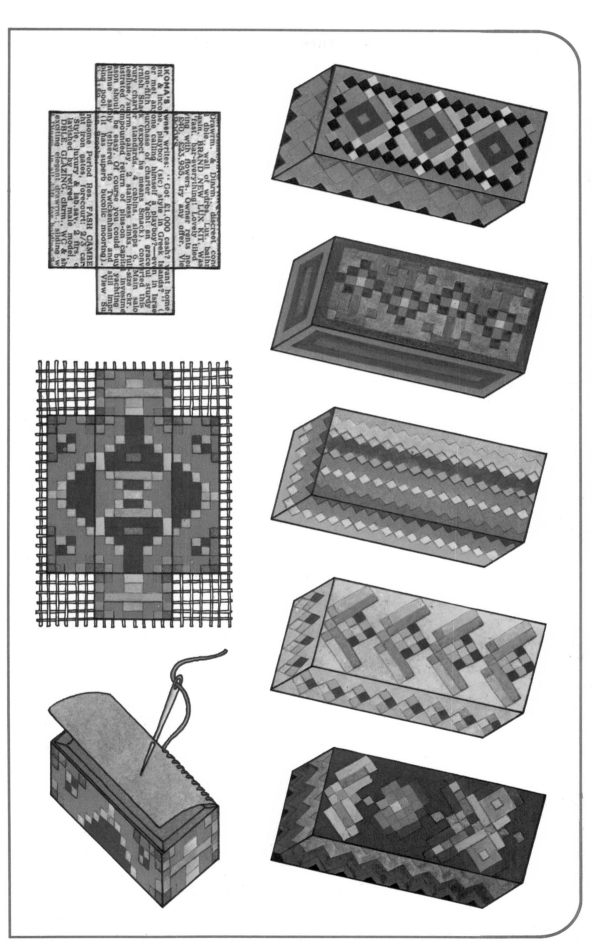

Making a lace pricking

Bobbin Lace 4

This chapter deals with making a pattern guide or lace pricking to work with, which is very important to the relatively inexperienced lace maker. Later, an expert can dispense with guide lines, but to begin with prickings can be bought ready-made or copied from charts such as those in previous Bobbin Lace chapters. The scale of a lace pricking can vary between eight and twelve squares to the inch on the graph paper, although at first it is easiest to work on the largest of these scales.

Preparing a pattern

You will need

- ☐ Graph paper 8 or 10 squares to the inch
- ☐ Thin art cardboard
- ☐ Pen
- ☐ Pin vice (or No.8 sewing needle inserted at the eye into a cork)

Mark out the dots on the graph paper. Place the prepared graph paper over the pricking cardboard. Blue or green is the best color to work on with art cardboard as it creates considerably less eye strain.

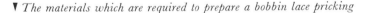

▼ *The materials which are required to prepare a bobbin lace pricking*

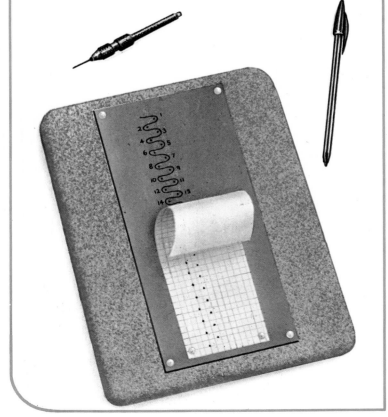

▲ *A souvenir doll from Brussels, one of the world's great lace-making cities*

Using the pin vice or needle, prick holes through the dots and the cardboard. Do not however, make the holes too big. You can work on the lace pillow, but a cork square, two cork table mats or a pad of thick felt give a flatter and more accurate surface to work on. Attach the graph paper and cardboard firmly to the working surface with thumbtacks.

Take the graph paper off the cardboard and ink in the lines of the pattern between the dots. For beginners the holes can be numbered as a guide to the order of the pattern. It is in these holes that the lace pins are placed.

Ready-prepared patterns, professionally known as prickings, can be bought from suppliers of lace materials.

Diagonal openwork stitch

Copy the chart as illustrated. Place 2 pairs of bobbins on points a, b, c, d, e, f.

Turn the 2nd pair twice and the 1st pair once, cross and fix with a pin on point 1 and make a half stitch.

Turn and cross the 3rd and 4th pairs, fix with a pin on point 2 and make a half stitch.

Turn and cross the 2nd and 3rd pairs, turn the 1st pair twice and the 2nd pair once, fix with a pin on point 3 and make a half stitch.

Turn and cross the 2nd and 3rd pairs, place a pin on point 4 and make a half stitch.

Turn and cross the 1st and 2nd pairs, fix with a pin on point 5 and make a half stitch.

*Turn the 6th pair twice and the 7th pair once, cross, fix with a pin on point 6 and make a half stitch.

Turn and cross the 7th and 8th pairs, fix with a pin on point 7 and make a half stitch.

Turn and cross the 6th and 7th pairs, turn the 5th pair twice and the 6th pair once, cross and fix with a pin on point 8 and make a half stitch.

Turn and cross the 6th and 7th pairs, fix with a pin on point 9 and make a half stitch.

Turn and cross the 5th and 6th pairs, turn the 4th pair twice and the 5th pair once, cross, fix

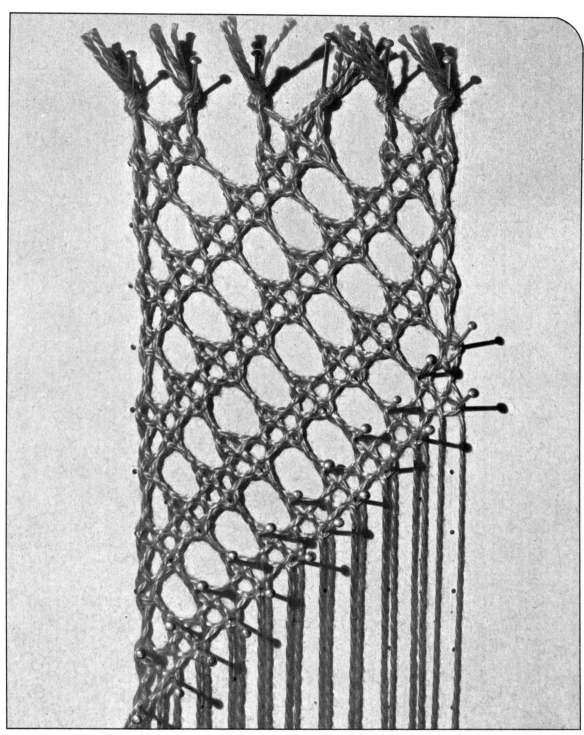

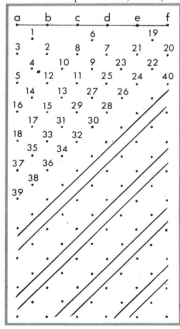

◄ *Diagonal openwork stitch chart*   ▲ *Diagonal openwork stitch which is worked on twenty-four bobbins*

with a pin on point 10 and make a half stitch.

Turn and cross the 5th and 6th pairs, fix with a pin on point 11 and make a half stitch.

Turn and cross the 4th and 5th pairs, turn the 3rd pair twice and the 4th pair once, cross, fix with a pin on point 12 and make a half stitch.

Turn and cross the 4th and 5th pairs, fix with a pin on point 13

and make a half stitch.

Turn and cross the 3rd and 4th pairs, turn the 2nd pair twice and the 3rd pair once, cross and fix with a pin on point 14 and make a half stitch.

Turn and cross the 3rd and 4th pairs, fix with a pin on point 15 and make a half stitch.

Turn and cross the 2nd and 3rd pairs, turn the 1st pair twice

and the 2nd pair once, cross and fix with a pin on point 16 and make a half stitch.

Turn and cross the 2nd and 3rd pairs, fix with a pin on point 17 and make a half stitch.

Turn and cross the 1st and 2nd pairs, fix with a pin on point 18 and make a half stitch.

Start again from * following the consecutive numbers on the chart.

Adaptable patterns for children's clothes

This chapter has adaptable graph patterns for day and night clothes for boys and girls from 3 to 7 years. Make the nightgown with short sleeves or turn the pajamas into long pants by making them as the shorts.

Boy's top and shorts

Sizing

For a boy aged 4 with 23in chest and 21in waist; aged 5 to 6 with 24in chest and 22in waist; aged 7 with 25in chest and 23in waist.

Suggested fabrics

Denim or sailcloth.

You will need:

☐ 1¾yd 36in wide fabric
☐ ¾yd ¾in wide elastic
☐ Two 1½in diameter metal rings for the belt or one 1in buckle
☐ Matching and contrasting thread
☐ Graph paper for patterns

The pattern

Copy pattern pieces numbers 1, 2, 3, 4, 5 and 6.

For the shorts copy the shorter length as shown on pattern piece number 1 and also draw in the side seam and cut the pattern along this line. Draw in the pocket position on the shorts Front.

Cutting out

Following figure **1**, lay out the pattern pieces on the fabric as shown.

The pattern has no seam or hem allowance, so add the amounts given with the graph.
1176

Cut out the fabric and also cut a belt (a) 30in by 3½in and two pockets (b) 6½in by 5½in.

Making the outfit

Shorts. Overcast one short edge of each pocket and then turn under for 1½ inches. Using contrasting thread make two rows of topstitching along this edge 1 inch and 1¼ inches from the fold. This edge becomes the top of the pocket.

On each pocket turn under the lower edge and the edge which goes nearest the Center Front for ⅜ inch. Baste the pockets in position on the front of the shorts, with the remaining raw edge of each pocket even with the raw edge of the side seam. Using contrasting thread top-stitch the pocket along the front and lower edge with two rows of stitches ¼ inch apart. Stitch the side seams, leg seams and crotch seams, in that order, using contrasting thread and flat-fell seaming on the outside of the garment.

Make ¾ inch hems on the leg edges and stitch with matching thread.

Cut a length of elastic to fit the boy's waist and join the narrow ends to form a circle. Turn in the waist edge ⅛ inch,

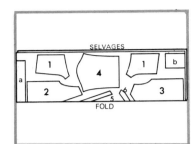

▲ **1.** *Layout: boy's top and shorts*

▲ *Details of boy's top and shorts*

then turn in again 1⅛ inch and place the elastic in the fold. Stitch the waist casing with matching thread; be careful not to stitch over the elastic. Smooth any fullness away at Center Front, then stitch through the casing and elastic 3 inches to each side of the Center Front seam to give a flat effect at the front (see front view of shorts).

Top. Using contrasting thread and flat-fell seaming stitch the shoulder seams, armhole seams (pressing the seams toward the sleeves), and the side seams and sleeve seams in one operation starting at the hem.

Using matching thread stitch ¾ inch hems on sleeves and top.

Join neck facings at shoulder seams and Center Front seam. Sew to neck edge with right sides facing, taking ¼ inch seams.

Snip seam allowance, then turn and topstitch (or understitch) the facing to the seam allowance.

Finish the raw edge of the facing then, using contrasting thread, topstitch to the top with two rows of stitches 1 inch and 1¼ inches from the neck edge working on the right side.

Belt. Fold in half lengthwise, right sides facing. Stitch, taking a ¼ inch seam and leaving an opening for turning. Turn to the right side and close the opening.

Press, then topstitch all around with contrasting thread making two rows of stitches ¼ inch apart.

Firmly stitch two rings or a buckle at one end.

Boy's pajamas

Sizing

As for top and shorts with the following outer leg lengths: 24in, 26in and 28in respectively.

Suggested fabrics

Soft cotton fabrics like flannelette; plissé.

You will need

☐ 1¼yd 36in wide fabric for top and 1½yd 36in wide for pants and trimmings
☐ ¾yd ¾in wide elastic
☐ Matching thread
☐ Graph paper for patterns

The pattern

Copy pattern pieces numbers 1, 2, 3, 4, 5, 6 and 7. The pants pattern piece 1 is drawn full length and without side seams.

Cutting out

Following figure 2, lay out the pattern pieces on the fabric as shown.

The pattern has no seam or hem allowances, so add the amounts given with the graph. Cut out the fabric.

Making the pajamas

Pants. Stitch the leg seams and crotch seams with flat-fell seaming on the outside of the fabric.

Stitch ¾ inch hems on the legs. Cut a length of elastic to fit the child's waist and join the narrow ends to form a circle.

▼ *2. Layout: boy's pajamas*

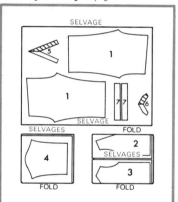

▼ *Details of boy's pajamas*

▲ *For the girl's smock, checked gingham with plain poplin—tough denim for the boy's top and shorts*

Turn in the waist edge ⅛ inch, then turn in again for 1⅛ inch and place elastic in the fold. Stitch the waist casing being careful not to stitch over the elastic.

Top. Stitch seams in sleeve-bands and neckband.

Stitch the shoulder, armhole, side and sleeve seams with flat-fell seaming. Press armhole seams toward the sleeves.

Stitch a sleeveband to each sleeve edge. To do this, place the right side of the band to the wrong side of the sleeve, with seams matching and raw edges even. Stitch with ¼ inch seam.

Press the seam allowances toward the sleeve and stitch to the sleeve very close to the hem edge. Do not stitch through the band at the same time.

Turn the sleeveband to the right side of the sleeve, turn under the raw edge to make the band 1¾ inches wide and topstitch close to the upper fold edge.

Stitch the neckband to the neck edge in the same way. But before topstitching in place, baste the neckband down making sure that the point is on the Center Front.

Girl's smock

Sizing
For a girl aged 3 with 22in chest; aged 4 to 5 with 23in chest; aged 6 with 24in chest.

Suggested fabrics
Gingham, poplin, denim or shirting.

You will need
- ☐ $1\frac{1}{4}$yd 36in wide main fabric and $\frac{1}{2}$yd 36in wide contrasting fabric
- ☐ $\frac{1}{2}$yd $\frac{1}{4}$in wide elastic
- ☐ Matching thread and contrasting topstitch thread for pocket detail
- ☐ Graph paper for patterns

The pattern
Copy pattern pieces numbers 1, 2, 3, 4 and 5 from the graph.

▼**3.** *Layout: girl's smock*

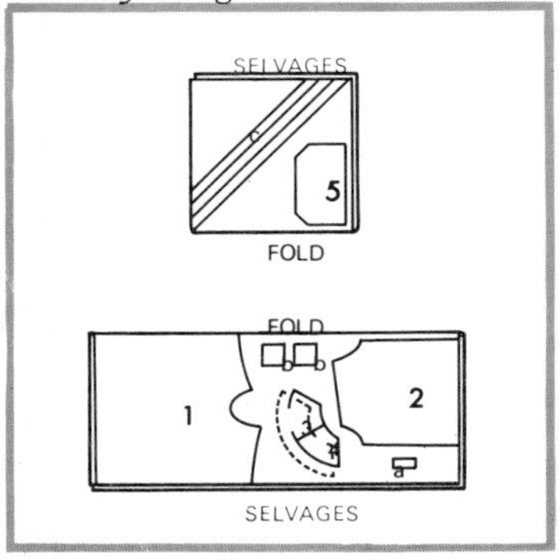

▼*Details of girl's smock*

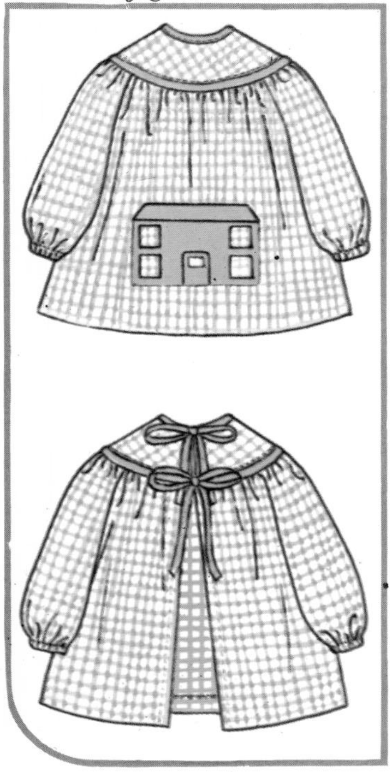

Cutting out
Following figure **3**, lay out the pattern pieces on the fabric as shown.
Make the other half of the Front yoke pattern and join them at the Center Front. Cut the yokes from single fabric as shown, with the Center Front and Center Backs on the crosswise grain of the fabric.
The pattern has no seam or hem allowances, so add the amounts given with the graph.
Cut out the fabric and also cut the following: from main fabric, one pocket window (a) $2\frac{1}{2}$in by $1\frac{1}{2}$in, and four pocket windows (b) $2\frac{1}{2}$in square; from contrasting fabric cut 3 yards of $1\frac{1}{4}$in wide bias strips (c) as shown.

Making the smock
Pocket. Place the pocket pieces together, right sides facing, and stitch around, leaving one side of the roof open Turn to the right side.
Using contrasting thread and a large stitch, topstitch the top and bottom of the roof and the door.
Turn in the raw edges of each window for $\frac{1}{4}$ inch all around and stitch them to the pocket.
Topstitch the pocket to the Front of the smock along the sides and lower edge. Backstitch the opening corners securely.
Sleeves. Stitch the sleeve seams with a French seam.
Stitch $\frac{1}{2}$ inch hems leaving openings for inserting elastic. Thread a $7\frac{1}{2}$ inch length elastic in each sleeve hem. Stitch ends of elastic firmly together and close the opening.
Stitch sleeves to skirt at underarm with a French seam and press seams toward sleeves.
Yoke. French seam the shoulders.
Bind Center Back edges of yoke with contrasting bias strip.
To do this, place the right side of binding to wrong side of Center Back, raw edges even. Stitch with $\frac{1}{4}$ inch seam. Fold binding to right side, turn in raw edge for $\frac{1}{4}$ inch and topstitch in place over the first row of stitching.
To bind neck edge, join two bias strips in the straight of grain to make up 1 yard. Stitch the binding to the wrong side of the neck edge as above, leaving 12 inches extending at each end to make ties.
Fold the binding to the right side.. Turn in $\frac{1}{4}$ inch along all raw edges, including the ties, and topstitch the folded binding from end to end.
Join bias strips to length of lower yoke edge plus 1 inch. Fold in half lengthwise, wrong sides together, turning in $\frac{1}{2}$ inch at each end to make neat. Place around lower edge of the yoke on right side, with the raw bias edge $\frac{1}{4}$ inch from yoke edge and bias fold upward.
Stitch in place $\frac{1}{2}$ inch from the lower yoke edge.
Skirt. Make two rows of gathering stitches $\frac{1}{4}$ inch and $\frac{1}{2}$ inch from the top edge of the skirt and sleeves, finishing the stitches $1\frac{1}{2}$ inches to each side of the Center Back.
Draw up to fit the yoke, matching notches to seams and leaving $\frac{1}{2}$ inch of skirt extending to each side of the Center Back. Pin, then stitch, taking a $\frac{5}{8}$ inch seam. Trim the seam allowance to $\frac{3}{8}$ inch and zigzag or overlock the raw edges together. Press the seam into the yoke. Topstitch through yoke and seam allowance close to seam.
Make a 1 inch hem on the skirt.
Fold in the Center Back edges $\frac{1}{2}$ inch and stitch down.
Make two 12 inch ties from the bias strips as for the neck ties and sew to the lower yoke edge at the Center Back.

Girl's nightgown

Sizing
As for girl's smock.

Suggested fabrics
Flannelette, brushed nylon, or seersucker.

You will need:
- ☐ $1\frac{3}{4}$yd of 36in wide fabric
- ☐ $3\frac{1}{2}$yd eyelet embroidery edging
- ☐ Shirring elastic
- ☐ 1 hook and eye, size No.1
- ☐ Matching thread
- ☐ Graph paper for patterns

The pattern
Copy pieces numbers 1, 2, 3 and 4.

Cutting out
Following figure **4**, lay out the pattern pieces on the fabric as shown.
The pattern has no seam or hem allowances, so add the amounts given with the graph.
Cut out the fabric and also cut a Front opening facing (a) 4in by $2\frac{1}{2}$in, two bias strips (b) $1\frac{1}{4}$in wide by 6in and two bias strips (c) $1\frac{1}{4}$in wide by 19in.
Cut a slit in the Center Front of the skirt 3 inches long from the neck edge.

Making the nightgown
Sleeves. With right sides facing, raw edges even, place eyelet embroidery trim on sleeve hem edges. Stitch, taking $\frac{1}{4}$ inch seams.
Press seam allowance on each upward, turn in the raw edges and stitch a $\frac{1}{8}$ inch hem. Stitch the sleeve seams with a French seam.
With shirring elastic in the bobbin and a large stitch length, work two rows of shirring on each sleeve, $\frac{1}{4}$ inch apart and starting 1 inch up from the top of the trim. Knot ends securely.
French seam the sleeves to the skirt at the underarm and press seam toward the sleeve.
Yoke. French seam the shoulders.
Cut three pieces of eyelet embroidery, one 31 inches long and two 7 inches long. Machine gather each piece $\frac{3}{16}$ inch from the raw edge.
Gather the short pieces to the depth of the yoke at the Center Front. Pin to the right side of each Front yoke piece, placing the raw edge of the trim $\frac{1}{2}$ inch from the Center Front. Topstitch in place over the gathering line then zigzag raw edge of trim flat to the yoke.
Gather up the 31 inch length to fit around the neck and Center Front edges. Pin in place to the right side with raw edges of yoke and trim even. Baste.
Using the short bias strips (b) bind both Center Front edges taking $\frac{1}{4}$ inch seams.

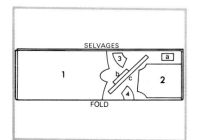

▲ **4.** *Layout: girl's nightgown*

▲ *Details of girl's nightgown*

▲ *Pretty printed cotton is first choice for the nightgown—flannelette in contrasting colors for the pajamas*

Join the long bias strips in the straight grain of the fabric. Place the strip centrally along the neck edge, with right sides facing, raw edges even. Stitch, taking a $\frac{1}{4}$ inch seam.

Stitch the strip extending at each end into a rouleau for the ties. Turn the rouleaux to the right side and complete the binding of neck edge.

Stay-stitch the yoke $\frac{1}{2}$ inch from the lower edge.

Gather remaining eyelet embroidery to fit lower yoke edge with the ends extending at Center Front. Pin to right side of yoke $\frac{1}{4}$ inch from yoke edge. Machine stitch in place along the gathering line.

Skirt. Stitch $\frac{1}{2}$in Center Back seam.

Make two rows of gathering stitches $\frac{1}{4}$ inch and $\frac{1}{2}$ inch from the top edge of the skirt and sleeves. Draw up to fit the yoke, matching notches to seams and leaving $\frac{1}{4}$ inch extending at both Front edges.

Stitch with $\frac{5}{8}$ inch seam. Trim seam allowance to $\frac{3}{8}$ inch and zigzag or overlock the edges together. Press seam upward. Make the raw edges of the facing neat, then pin the facing centrally over the Center Front opening with right sides together. Stitch with $\frac{1}{4}$ inch seam graduating to nothing at the point to each side of the Center Front opening. Slash between the stitching. Understitch the seam allowance to the facing then turn to the inside.

Hand sew the top edges of facing to yoke seam and sew on a hook and eye at this point. Make a 1 inch hem on the skirt.

▼ Graph pattern: girl's smock and nightgown

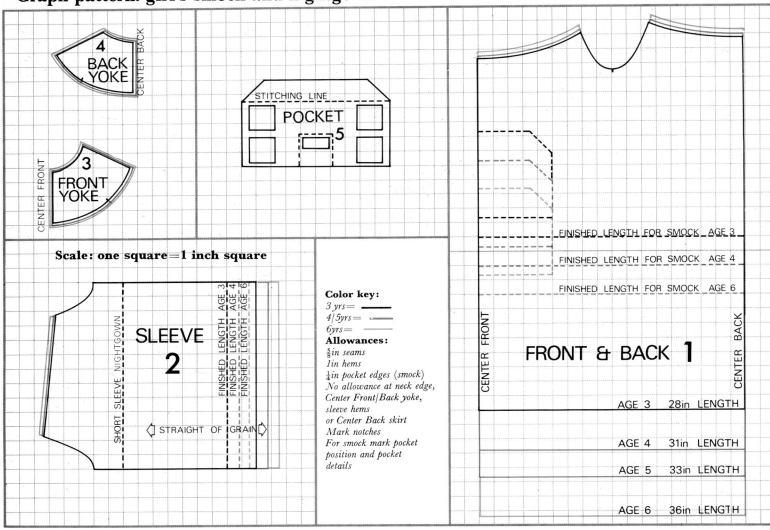

4 BACK YOKE — CENTER BACK

3 FRONT YOKE — CENTER FRONT

STITCHING LINE

POCKET 5

Scale: one square = 1 inch square

SLEEVE 2

SHORT SLEEVE NIGHTGOWN

FINISHED LENGTH AGE 3 / FINISHED LENGTH AGE 4 / FINISHED LENGTH AGE 6

◁ STRAIGHT OF GRAIN ▷

Color key:
3 yrs = ▬▬▬
4/5 yrs = ▬▬▬
6 yrs = ▬▬▬

Allowances:
⅝ in seams
1 in hems
¼ in pocket edges (smock)
No allowance at neck edge,
Center Front/Back yoke,
sleeve hems
or Center Back skirt
Mark notches
For smock mark pocket
position and pocket
details

FINISHED LENGTH FOR SMOCK AGE 3
FINISHED LENGTH FOR SMOCK AGE 4
FINISHED LENGTH FOR SMOCK AGE 6

CENTER FRONT

FRONT & BACK 1

CENTER BACK

AGE 3   28 in LENGTH

AGE 4   31 in LENGTH

AGE 5   33 in LENGTH

AGE 6   36 in LENGTH

▼ Graph pattern: boy's top and shorts, and pajamas

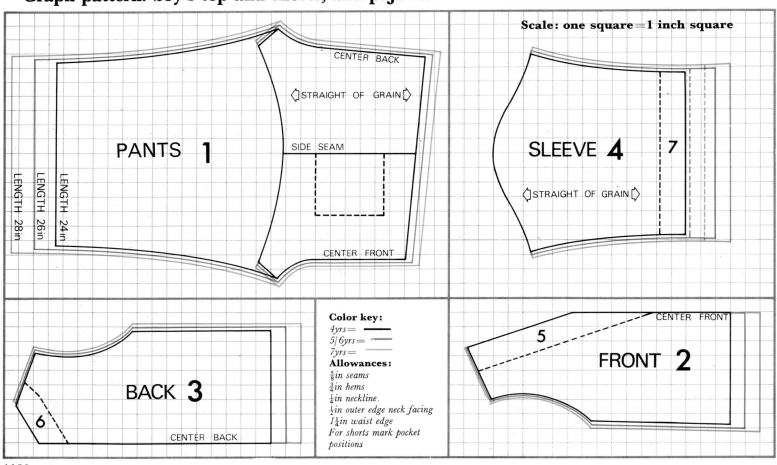

Scale: one square = 1 inch square

CENTER BACK

◁ STRAIGHT OF GRAIN ▷

SIDE SEAM

PANTS 1

LENGTH 28 in / LENGTH 26 in / LENGTH 24 in

CENTER FRONT

SLEEVE 4 7

◁ STRAIGHT OF GRAIN ▷

BACK 3

6

CENTER BACK

Color key:
4 yrs = ▬▬▬
5/6 yrs = ▬▬▬
7 yrs = ▬▬▬

Allowances:
⅝ in seams
¾ in hems
¼ in neckline
½ in outer edge neck facing
1¼ in waist edge
For shorts mark pocket
positions

CENTER FRONT

5

FRONT 2

Pattern Library

Teneriffe lace mat

This pretty mat is made of eight Teneriffe lace motifs applied around a fabric center. Each motif is made up of fifty petals held in place by three concentric circles of knotting, and each is partially joined to the next and buttonhole stitched to the linen. The center of the mat is drawn threadwork with webs formed across the spaces. Spirals of knotting hold the webs in position and two rows of four sided stitch surround the entire centerpiece. The lace is in matte embroidery cotton.

Looped, striped and lacy pillows

Three rich-looking knitted pillow patterns and an opportunity for you to practice your knitting techniques.

Looped effects

The looped pillow can also be given a different appearance by working several rows of one color, then changing to a contrast of a different shade of the first color. For example, gradual shading toward the center would give a flower-like appearance.

Garter stitch

The garter stitch square can be used in various different ways to give a variety of effects both in the arrangements of the squares and in the mixing of self-colored squares with striped squares. Color effects can also give different appearances to the same arrangement of squares.

Lace effects

Try different lace effects (see Knitting Know-how chapters 29, page 562 and 41, page 802) for suitable stitches or experiment with the color of the pillow lining beneath the lace pattern. A strong contrast will emphasize the lace effect.

Loop pillow

Size

Approx 17in diameter, adjustable as desired.

Gauge
4 sts and 7 rows to 1in over garter st worked on No.8 needles.

Materials

Reynolds La Quality No.1 Mohair
5 40gm balls
One pair No.8 needles
(or Canadian No.5)
One round 18in foam form

Base

Begin at center.
Cast on 9 sts.
1st and every other row K.
2nd row Inc in each st to last st, K1.
4th row *K1, inc, rep from * to last st, K1.
6th row *K2, inc, rep from * to last st, K1.
8th row *K3, inc, rep from * to last st, K1.
10th row *K4, inc, rep from * to last st, K1.
Continue inc in this way until work measures 8½in from cast-on edge. Bind off.

Top

Begin at center. Cast on 9 sts.

1st row K1, * insert needle as if to K and wind yarn over needle point and 2 fingers twice, then around needle point and draw loops through, return to left-hand needle and K tog tbl loops and original st—called ML—, K1, rep from * to end.
2nd row Inc in each st to last st, K1.
3rd and every other row K1, *ML, K1, rep from * to end.
4th row *K1, inc, rep from * to last st, K1.
6th row *K2, inc, rep from * to last st, K1.
8th row *K3, inc, rep from * to last st, K1.
Continue inc in this way on every other row 8 times, working loop row on odd rows.
Work until the same size as base.

Finishing

Seam edges leaving an opening for foam form.
Insert form and close opening.

Garter stitch pillow

Size

16in square.

Gauge
5½ sts and 7½ rows to 1in over stockinette stitch worked on No.5 needles.

Materials

Reynolds Classique, 50grm balls
6 balls main color A, white
1 ball contrast color B, tan
1 ball contrast color C, red
1 ball contrast color D, black
One pair No.5 needles
(or Canadian No.8)
16in square foam form

Front

Using No.5 needles and A, cast on 3 sts.
1st row K.
2nd row Inc by K twice into same st, inc, K1.
3rd row K.
4th row Inc, K2, inc, K1.
5th row K.
Continue inc in this way inside the edge sts on next and every other row until there are 31 sts.
Break off A. Keeping inc correct as before, work 12 rows B, 12 rows C, 12 rows D. Break off D and complete with A. 67 sts. K 1 row.
Dec one st at each side inside edge sts, on next and every other row until 3 sts rem. K 1 row. Bind off.
Work 3 more squares in the same way. Join squares together, matching stripes carefully.

Back

Work as given for Front, using A only for each square.

Finishing

Seam Back and Front together, leaving one side open. Insert foam form and slip stitch remaining side tog.

Lacy pillow

Size

12in by 17in.

Gauge
6 sts and 8 rows to 1in over stockinette stitch worked on No.6 needles.

Materials

Reynolds Wendy Whisper
14 25gm balls
One pair No.6 needles
(or Canadian No.7)
12in by 17in foam form

Note

To work Tw2F and Tw2B, see Knitting Know-how chapter 16, page 302.

Front

Using No.6 needles, cast on 67 sts.
K5 rows.
Commence patt.
1st row K1, *Tw2F, K4, ytf, sl 1, K1, psso, K3, Tw2B, rep from * to last st, K1.
2nd and every other row K1, P to last st, K1.
3rd row K1, *Tw2F, K2, K2 tog, ytf, K1, ytf, sl 1, K1, psso, K2, Tw2B, rep from * to last st, K1.
5th row K1, *Tw2F, K1, K2 tog, ytf, K3, ytf, sl 1, K1, psso, K1, Tw2B, rep from * to last st, K1.
7th row K1, *Tw2F, K2 tog, ytf, K5, ytf, sl 1, K1, psso, Tw2B, rep from * to last st, K1.
8th row As 2nd.
Rep these 8 rows 11 times more.
K5 rows. Bind off.

Back

Work as given for Front.

Finishing

Join seams on 3 sides. Insert foam form and slip stitch remaining side closed.
If desired, make 4 large tassels and attach one to each corner.

The garter stitch pillow square with its three-color diagonal band can be grouped in a variety of ways ▶

The flash finish dress

Knitted circularly so that there are no side seams, the skirt of this scoop-necked dress, in a pretty lacy stitch, hangs particularly well. The sleeves are raglan-shaped, and are finished with a ribbed cuff to match the neckline edge.

Sizes

Directions are for 34in bust. The figures in brackets [ ] refer to the 36, 38 and 40in sizes respectively.

Length from shoulder to lower edge, 45[46¾:48½:50¼]in, adjustable.

Sleeve seam, 12½[12½:13½:13½] in.

Gauge

7½ sts and 9½ rows to 1in over stockinette stitch worked on No.3 needles.

Materials

Unger Cruise
10[11:12:14]
1·4/10oz balls
One No.3 circular needle (or Canadian No.10)
29in long
One No.2 circular needle (or Canadian No.11)
14in long
One large stitch holder

Dress

Begin at lower edge of skirt. Using 29in No.3 circular needle cast on 396[432:468:504]sts. Work back and forth.

1st row *K1, P1, rep from * to end.

2nd row *P1, K1, rep from * to end.

Rep these 2 rows 5 times more.
1184

Join work into a circle and continue in rounds. Place marker thread at beginning of round.

1st round *K4; ytf, K4, sl 1, K2 tog, psso, K4, ytf, K3, rep from * to end of round.

2nd and every other round K.

3rd round *K5, ytf, K3, sl 1, K2 tog, psso, K3, ytf, K4, rep from * to end of round.

5th round *K6, ytf, K2, sl 1, K2 tog, psso, K2, ytf, K5, rep from * to end of round.

7th round *K7, ytf, K1, sl 1, K2 tog, psso, K1, ytf, K6, rep from * to end of round.

9th round *K4, (ytf, sl 1, K2 tog, psso, ytf, K1) 3 times, K2, rep from * to end of round.

10th round K.

These 10 rounds form patt. Rep 1st—10th rounds 7[8:9:10] times more. If the length is to be altered, work more or fewer patterns at this point, allowing 1in for each patt. Work the 1st patt round once.

1st dec round *K2 tog, K16, rep from * to end of round. 374[408:442:476] sts.

Next round *K4, ytf, K3, sl 1, K2 tog, psso, K3, ytf, K4, rep from * to end of round.

Continue in patt as established, noting that 1 less st is worked at the beg of each patt rep. Work until 5 more patts have been completed, then work 1st patt round skipping last K st of round.

2nd dec round *K2 tog, K15, rep from * to end of round.

352[384:416:448] sts.

Next round *K4, ytf, K3, sl 1, K2 tog, psso, K3, ytf, K3, rep from * to end of round. Continue in patt as established, working 1 st less at beg and end of each patt rep until 3 more patts have been completed. Work 1st patt round once.

3rd dec round *K2 tog, K14, rep from * to end. 330[360:390:420] sts.

Next round *K3, ytf, K3, sl 1, K2 tog, psso, K3, ytf, K3, rep from * to end of round. Continue in patt as established, working 2 sts less at beg and 1 st less at end of each patt rep until 3 complete patts have been worked. Work 1st patt round once, skipping last K st.

4th dec round *K2 tog, K13, rep from * to end. 308[336:364:392] sts.

Next round *K3, ytf, K3, sl 1, K2 tog, psso, K3, ytf, K2, rep from * to end of round. Continue in patt as established, working 2 sts less at each end of every patt rep until 3 more patts have been completed. Work 1st patt round once.

5th dec round *K2 tog, K12, rep from * to end. 286[312:338:364] sts.

Next round *K2, ytf, K3, sl 1, K2 tog, psso, K3, ytf, K2, rep from * to end. Continue in patt as established, working 3 sts less at beg and 2 sts less at end of each patt rep until 3 more patts have been completed. Work 1st patt round once, skipping last K st and ending with ytf.

6th dec round *K2 tog, K11, rep from * to end of round. 264[288:312:336] sts.

Next round *K2, ytf, K3, sl 1, K2 tog, psso, K3, ytf, K1, rep from * to end of round. Continue in patt as established, working 3 sts less at each end of every patt rep until work measures 30[31:32:33]in, or desired length to waist.

Change to different patt which is used throughout bodice and sleeves.

1st round *K1, ytf, K4,

sl 1, K2 tog, psso, K4, ytf, rep from * to end of round.

2nd and every other round K.

3rd round K2, *ytf, K3, sl 1, K2 tog, psso, K3, ytf, K3, rep from * to end of round ending with K1 instead of K3.

5th round K2 tog, *ytf, K1, ytf, K2, sl 1, K2 tog, psso, K2, ytf, K1, ytf, sl 1, K2 tog, psso, rep from * to last 10 sts, ytf, K1, ytf, K2, sl 1, K2 tog, psso, K2, ytf, K2 tog, ytf.

7th round *Ytf, sl 1, K1, psso, K2, ytf, K1, sl 1, K2 tog, psso, K1, ytf, K3, rep from * to end of round.

9th round K1, *ytf, sl 1, K2 tog, psso, ytf, K1, rep from * to end of round, skipping last K st.

10th round K.

These 10 rounds form the bodice patt.

Rep 1st—10th rounds once more.

Inc round Inc for the sides as follows: *inc in first st, work in patt until 11[12:13:14] patts have been worked, inc in last st*, rep from * to * thus increasing 2 sts at each side.

Marker threads placed at each inc will make counting easier. Work 9 rounds patt, knitting the extra inc sts.

Rep last 10 rounds 3 times more. 8 sts have now been increased at each side. Mark beg of round in center of 8 st panel 4 sts in.

Work without shaping until work measures 39[40¼:41½:42¾]in, ending after a K round.

Shape front raglan armholes

1st row Bind off 4 sts, work in patt until 11[12:13:14] patts have been worked, K4, turn and work back and forth on these sts only.

2nd row Bind off 4 sts, P to end.

3rd row K2, sl 1, K1, psso, work to last 4 sts, K2 tog, K2.

4th row P.

Rep last 2 rows 3[5:7:9] times more.

Shape front neck

1st row K2, sl 1, K1, psso, patt 40[43:46:49] sts, turn and work on these sts only.
2nd row P.
3rd row K2, sl 1, K1, psso, patt to last 2 sts, K2 tog.
4th row P.
Rep last 2 rows 3[4:5:6] times more.
**Continue to dec at armhole edge on next and every RS row; *at the same time* dec one st at neck edge on every 4th row until 21[16:23:18] sts rem. Continue to dec at armhole edge as before, but keep neck edge straight until 3 sts rem, P3. Bind off.
With RS facing, sl first 36 [38:40:42] sts on stitch holder, attach yarn to rem sts.
1st row Patt to last 4 sts, K2 tog, K2.
2nd row P.
3rd row Dec one st, patt to last 4 sts, K2 tog, K2.
4th row Rep last 2 rows 3[4:5:6] times more.
Complete as for first side, working from ** to end.

Shape back raglan armholes

With RS facing, attach yarn to rem sts, bind off 4 sts at beg of next 2 rows.
3rd row K2, sl 1, K1, psso, patt to last 4 sts, K2 tog, K2.
4th row P.
Rep last 2 rows 6[8:10:12] times more.

Shape back neck

1st row K2, sl 1, K1, psso, patt 34[37:40:43], turn and work on these sts only.
2nd row P.
3rd row K2, sl 1, K1, psso, patt to last 2 sts, K2 tog.
4th row P.
Rep last 2 rows 0[1:2:4] times more. Complete from ** of first side of front neck to end.
With RS of work facing, sl first 42[44:46:48] sts onto a st holder, attach yarn to rem sts and work to correspond to other side.

Sleeves

Using 14in No.2 circular needle, cast on 74[74:86:86] sts. Work back and forth

throughout sleeve.
Work 16 rows K1, P1 rib.
Change to 29in No.3 circular needle. Work in patt as given for bodice adding 1 K st at each end to allow for seaming.
1st row K1, *K1, ytf, K4, sl 1, K2 tog, psso, K4, ytf, rep from * to last st, K1.
2nd row P.
Continue in patt as established until 10th row has been completed, then inc one st at each end of next and every 6th row until there are 98 [102:106:110] sts, working the inc sts into patt as they are made.
Work without further shaping until sleeve measures 12½[12½: 13½:13½]in, ending with a P row.

Shape cap

Bind off 4 sts at beg of next 2 rows.
3rd row K2, sl 1, K1, psso, patt to last 4 sts, K2 tog, K2.
4th row P.
Rep last 2 rows until 18 sts rem. Slip sts on st holder for neck ribbing.

Finishing

Press each piece lightly on WS under damp cloth using warm iron. Join sleeve seams. Sew sleeve into armhole.
Slip the 42[44:46:48] sts from back st holder onto 29in No.3 circular needle, slip sts from one sleeve cap onto needle, slip 36[38:40:42] sts from front and sts from second sleeve cap all onto same needle. Attach yarn to end of 18 sts of right sleeve and pick up and K34 sts to st holder, rib 42[44:46: 48] sts from holder, then pick up and K34 sts to left sleeve, rib 18 sts sleeve and pick up and K66 sts to stitch holder, rib 36[38:40:42] sts from holder, pick up and K66 sts to right sleeve and rib 18 sts from sleeve. 314[318:322: 326] sts. Join sts.
Work in rounds of K1, P1 rib for 12 rounds. Bind off in rib.

Above left: a charming dress knitted in a fine lace pattern
Below left: a close-up detail of the lace pattern

Making good use of motifs

Some of the motifs which have been given in previous chapters can be used to make pretty accessories and trims if the motifs are worked using a fine cotton and hook. Here are six of the motifs, directions for working them into charming accessories and trims, and some more amusing ways with trims to work out for yourself.

Earrings and choker

Size
To fit average adult. The choker can be adjusted as necessary.

> **Gauge**
> Large motif measures about 2in.
> Small motif measures about 1½in.

Materials required
Clark's Big Ball Mercerized Crochet, 3 cord, size 30
1 350 yd ball
One No.B (2.00 mm) crochet hook
2 earring clips
2 small hooks and eyes

Choker
Using No.B crochet hook, work neckband. Ch8.
1st row Into 2nd ch from hook work 1sc, *1sc into next ch, rep from * to end. Turn.
2nd row Ch1, *1sc into next sc, rep from * to end. Turn.
Rep 2nd row until neckband measures 12in or desired length.
Fasten off.
Central motif. Work as for large rosebud (see Crochet

1186

Know-how chapter 49, p. 966), working 1st-8th rounds only.
Sew to center of neckband.
Side motifs. Work 4 motifs as given for small rosebud (see Crochet Know-how chapter 49).
Sew 2 motifs at either side of central motif. Sew hooks and eyes to ends of neckband.

Earrings
Work 2 motifs as given for small rosebud (see Crochet Know-how chapter 49).
Sew one motif to each clip.

Headband

Size
To fit any size.

> **Gauge**
> Motif measures approx 2¼in.

You will need
Coats & Clark's O.N.T. Pearl Cotton
1 50 yd ball
One No.B (2.00 mm) crochet hook
Short length elastic

Headband
Work rose motif as given for cameo center (see Crochet Know-how chapter 47, page 926). Work the number required to fit around head, omitting a small length for elastic under hair, about 4in.
Sew motifs together.
Sew elastic to ends, thus forming a circle.

Left-hand page: Choker and earrings, sweater yoke decoration, a headband, blouse decoration and an idea for trimming an evening skirt ►

Sweater yoke

> **Gauge**
> Motif measures about 3½in

Materials required
Oddments of sports weight yarn
One No.B (2.00 mm) crochet hook

Yoke
Work motif as given for star motif (see Crochet Know-how chapter 12, page 226). Work 7 motifs. Fasten off.

Fold 1 in. at each end of ribbon to wrong side and slip stitch into place.
Sew motifs onto ribbon.

Cover rings (see Crochet Know-how chapter 7, p. 126) and sew on ends of ribbon.

Work chain desired length to thread through rings.

Evening skirt trim

Wagon wheel motifs (see Crochet Know-how chapter 11, page 206) worked in glitter yarn or in rainbow colors can make a plain skirt into a party stealer.

For the lowest row of wheels, work the large wheel as given. For the second row, work 2 rounds fewer and for the third row work the small filler circles in one color only.
Fasten off ends, sew to skirt.

Belt

Size
To fit 27in waist, adjustable.

> **Gauge**
> Motif measures approx 3¼in.

You will need
Coats & Clark's O.N.T. Speed-Cro-Sheen
2 100yd balls of each color
One No. B (2.00 mm) crochet hook

Right-hand page: Belt, the earring motif on shoes and gloves, head-scarf with same motif on handbag, headband motif on a hat and scarf

29in of wide grosgrain ribbon or desired length plus 2in
2 plastic curtain rings

Belt
Work lace star motif (see Crochet Know-how 15, page 283). For two-color version work 1st and 2nd rounds in contrast and rem rounds in main color. Work sufficient motifs to fit around garment. Fasten off ends.

Sew securely in place.
The illustration shows the motifs placed in a semicircle but they could be placed at random or follow a neckline.

Headscarf

Size
To fit average adult head, adjustable.

> **Gauge**
> Motif measures approx 1½in square.

Materials required
Coats & Clark's O.N.T. Pearl Cotton
4 50 yd. balls
One No. B (2.00 mm) crochet hook
One small button

Headscarf
Work Forget-me-not motif (see Crochet Know-how chapter 13, page 246).
Work 78 motifs. Sew them together at corners only. Join 12 for front edge, 11 on second row placing them between those on the first row. Continue in this way forming a triangle. The numbers can be altered for a different size.

If preferred, the points on the front edge can be folded back and sewn in place to give a straight edge. Work a button loop on one corner of front edge and sew button to other corner.

Motifs for decoration
Motifs can be used to make garments but they can also be used to add interest to existing garments, giving a note of color or new life to an old favorite.

Patchwork dingle-dangle pets

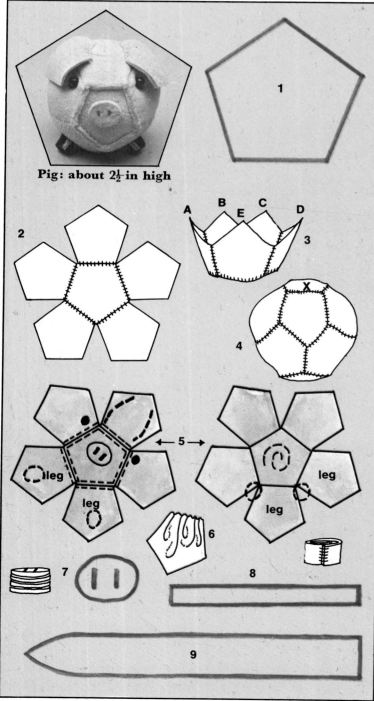

Pig: about 2½ in high

2

A B E C D

3

4

X

5

leg

leg

leg

leg

6

7

8

9

Simply made from patchwork, you can, if you wish, easily turn these little toys into mobiles. Tracing patterns are given for the shapes.

The basic shape
The basic shape for all the toys is made from pentagonal patches with 1 inch sides. The tracing pattern (figure **1**) gives the shape for all the patches. Using tracing paper, trace the pentagon from figure **1** and cut it out. Pin the tracing paper pattern to a piece of stiff cardboard and cut the pentagon from the cardboard. This is the template for all the patches and is used to cut papers for the patchwork toys when they are needed.

Each toy consists basically of a patchwork ball made from 12 pentagonal patches. The patches are joined first to each side of the central patch as shown in figure **2**. The sides of the outer patches are then joined together (figure **3**). A further five patches are joined along their sides between points A, B, C, D and E (figure **3**), leaving a pentagonal opening at X through which to insert the stuffing. The ball is completed by sewing the 12th patch into the opening (figure **4**).

The patches are joined together in the traditional way (right sides facing, whipped along the edge), but occasionally a patch will be sewn in with a stab stitch from the right side so that a ridged seam is obtained. Assembly diagrams are given for each toy showing the patches in two groups of six. This is in order to make clear the positioning for legs, ears, eyes, and other features. Tracing patterns are given for the features in each case.

The little pig

You will need
- [ ] 8in square chamois leather
- [ ] Scraps of black felt
- [ ] 1 pipe cleaner
- [ ] 2 small round black beads
- [ ] Matching sewing threads
- [ ] Contrasting embroidery floss
- [ ] Embroidery needle
- [ ] Fine needle
- [ ] Sharp scissors
- [ ] Rubber cement
- [ ] Kapok (a half pound will be more than enough to fill both toys)
- [ ] Pentagonal cardboard template

Assembling the pig
Follow figure **5** as your assembly diagram throughout.

Using the template cut 14 pentagons from the chamois leather. Gather and pull up the tops of 2 pentagons for the ears (figure **6**). Put 1 more pentagon aside and whip all the others together to make the basic shape. Turn right side out and stuff with kapok. Stab stitch the last pentagon into place from the outside, adding a little more kapok before finally closing up.

Nose. Cut 4 nose shapes from chamois leather (figure **7**). Embroider nostrils on the top one, glue all 4 nose shapes together one on top of the other, and glue the nose to the face where shown in figure **5**.

Eyes. Sew a round black bead into each eye position, passing the needle through the head and pulling the eyes together slightly.

Ears. Sew the 2 gathered patches into position where indicated in figure **5**.

Feet. Cut 4 strips of black felt each 2 inches long and ¼ inch wide. Place a little glue on one side of each strip and roll them up. Sew the ends to secure (figure **8**). Embroider cloven hoof marks onto each rolled up foot with contrasting embroidery floss. Glue each foot into position and sew them on using invisible stitches.

Tail. Cut the pipe cleaner in half. Cut a piece of chamois leather 3½ inches long and ½ inch wide and cut one end into a point (figure **9**).

Lay the pipe cleaner along the strip and overcast the chamois around it with matching thread keeping one end pointed. Twist the finished tail around a pencil to make a corkscrew then sew the blunt end into position, fixing it firmly to the body with invisible stitches.

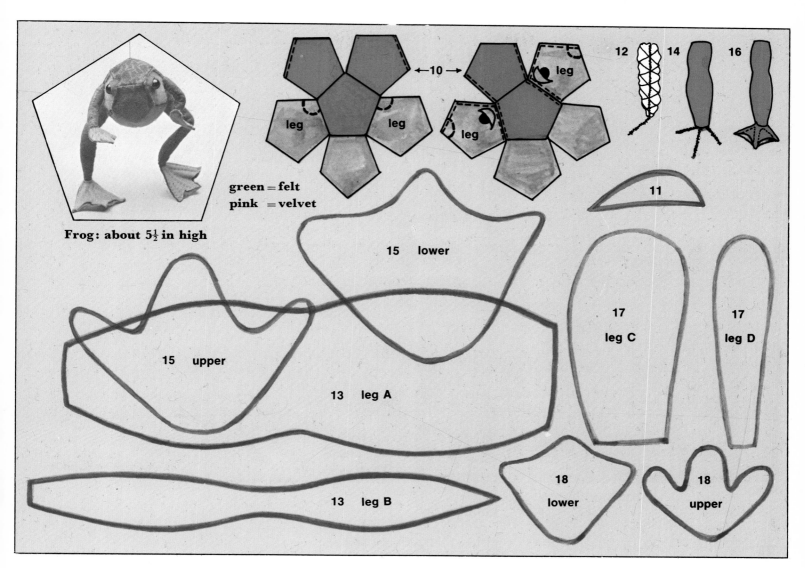

Frog: about 5½ in high

green = felt
pink = velvet

12 14 16

10

leg leg leg leg leg

11

15 lower

15 upper

13 leg A

13 leg B

17 leg C

17 leg D

18 lower

18 upper

Frog

You will need

- ☐ Scraps of pink and green felt
- ☐ Scraps of purple printed velvet
- ☐ 6 pipe cleaners
- ☐ 2 large round black beads
- ☐ Matching sewing threads
- ☐ Fine needle
- ☐ Scissors
- ☐ Kapok (for stuffing)
- ☐ Small roll of absorbent cotton (for padding the legs)
- ☐ Rubber cement
- ☐ Pentagonal cardboard template
- ☐ 5 pentagonal papers

Assembling the frog

Follow figure **10** as your assembly diagram throughout.

Using the template, from the felt cut 2 pink and 5 green patches. Cut 5 patches in printed velvet with ½ inch seam allowances, and baste these to the papers, turning in the seam allowances (see Patchwork chapter 1, page 332).

Whip the patches together to make the basic shape. Stab stitch three sides of each eye patch into place but leave two sides of one of the eye patches open for stuffing. Remove the papers and stuff the body with kapok, then finish stitching the eye patch in position.

Eyes. Sew the round black beads into place for the eyes as given for the little pig. Cut 2 eyelids (figure **11**) from green felt, and cement and sew these into position.

The back legs. Take 2 pipe cleaners. Bend one up, 1½ inches from the end. Wrap a little absorbent cotton around the remaining 4½ inches of the pipe cleaner and hold it in place with sewing thread wound loosely around it (figure **12**).

Cut 1 leg piece A from the printed velvet (figure **13**). Place the padded part of the pipe cleaner down the center of the wrong side of the leg piece A. Overcast the edges of the leg piece together and turn in the bottom edge to make it neat.

Take the other pipe cleaner and cut 4½ inches from this. Twist it around the end of the pipe cleaner protruding from the leg piece to form a claw (see figure **14**).

The webbed feet. Cut one green lower foot and one pink upper foot piece from felt (figure **15**).

Place the green lower foot piece beneath the claw and the upper foot piece above the claw. Sew around the claw with running stitches, enclosing it and forming a webbed foot. Sew the foot to lower leg edge (figure **16**).

Cut one green felt leg piece B (see figure **13**) and sew it into position with tiny stitches, hiding the seam down the back of the leg.

Repeat the whole process for the other back leg.

Front legs. Take the remaining 2 pipe cleaners and cut them in half, making four 3 inch lengths. Use 2 of these lengths to make the front legs (bending up 1 inch) and the other 2 to make the claws using the same method as for the back legs. Figures **17** and **18** give tracing patterns for the front leg pieces C and D, and feet.

To complete the frog, sew the front and back legs firmly into position where marked on figure **10**.

Spinning wheels of color

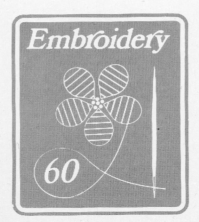

Embroidery 60

Color and stitch details are given for working this wool embroidered panel which is illustrated lifesize. Hang the panel framed or unframed.

To make this panel, finished size 18in by 12in, you will need:
- ½yd unbleached muslin
- ½yd green-colored twill weave fabric
- Hardboard for mounting
- Tapestry needle No. 18
- Crewel needle No. 5 or 6
- D.M.C. Tapestry yarn colors (1 skein of each) 7603, 7155, 7317, 7996, 7576, 7157, 7769, 7153, 7547, 7257, 7708, 7768, 7595, 7896, 7135, 7492, 7542, 7106, 7895, 7387
- Curtain rings
- D.M.C. Coton à Broder in colors (1 skein of each): 2227, 2825, 2572, 2209, 2570, 2595
- Rya wool (1 skein of each) in mauve, slate, turquoise and royal blue

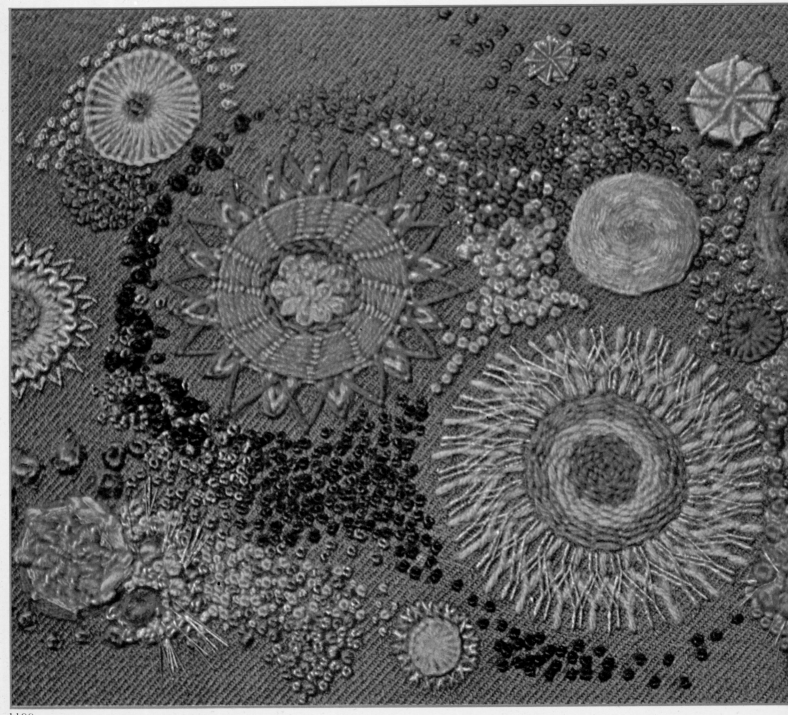

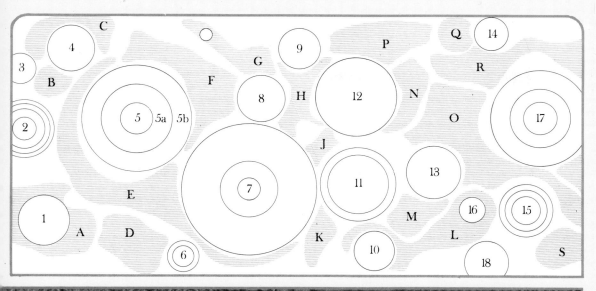

Trace design from the color picture and use the key as a guide to the yarns and stitches.

Circles

Instructions and colors are worked from center of circles. Numbers refer to D.M.C. Tapestry yarn colors unless otherwise stated.

1. *Spiders web framework: coton à broder/backweaving, Rya wool mauve, turquoise edged 7708.* **2.** *Chain stitch 7317/detached chain 7996/fly stitch 7153 and coton à broder 2595.* **3.** *Spiders web. Backweave 7257 and 7708.* **4.** *Buttonhole stitch 7996/straight stitches 7155.* **5.** *Detached rosette chain 7603/edged chain stitch 7157.* **5a.** *Circular couching 7155/with 7996.* **5b.** *Overlapping fly stitches 7157, 7106.* **6.** *Buttonhole stitch 7603/herringbone stitch 7155.* **7.** *Chain stitch 7155/spider web weaving 7996, 7317/slanting Cretan stitch 7576, 7155/sewing thread bright pink.* **8.** *Spiders web, 7708, 7996, 7896, 7603, 7135.* **9.** *Curtain ring buttonholed 7155/spiders web 7153, 7542.* **10.** *Spiders web 7153/fly stitches 7708.* **11.** *Curtain ring covered Rya wool mauve/chain stitch slate/detached rosette chain 7996.* **12.** *French knots 7542, 7996, 7547, 2 strands Rya wool royal blue couched around 7769.* **13.** *Spiders web 7603, 7106, 7155, 7257.* **14.** *Backweave spiders web/French knots 7603/weaving 7708, 7603.* **15.** *Knots 7542/chain stitch 7603, 7153.* **16.** *Spiders web 7542.* **17.** *French knots, 7996, 7595/weaving 7708/backweaving 7153, 7996.* **18.** *Curtain ring buttonholed 7708/spiders web 7603, 7317.*

French knot areas

The heaped areas of French knots are shaded on the chart. **A.** *Rya wool royal blue/fly stitch and French knots, coton à broder 2227, Rya wool mauve, turquoise.* **B.** *7317, 7157.* **C.** *Coton à broder 2825/sewing thread fly stitches.* **D.** *7895, 7996, 7317.* **E.** *7387, 7547, 7769, 7768.* **F.** *7153, 7603, 7896.* **G.** *7895/ scattering 7257.* **H.** *Rya wool mauve.* **J.** *Rya wool royal blue.* **K.** *7106, 7155, 7708.* **L.** *7153, 7708, coton à broder 2570.* **M.** *The same.* **N.** *Spaced knots 7996.* **O.** *7769, 7768, 7547, 7492.* **P.** *7542, 7576, 7317, 7996.* **Q.** *7708, 7603.* **R.** *7708, 7603.* **S.** *Rya wool royal blue, 7603, 7542, 7317, 7157.*

Collector's Piece

Influence of India

From the days of Marco Polo, the art of the east has influenced western embroidery and textile design. As trade links became more firmly established with China and India, the art of those countries flooded into the western world and embroiderers turned more frequently to eastern textiles and engravings for their inspiration. Elizabethan embroidery designs, for instance, are mostly floral with a pleasing balance between naturalism and formality. Similar leaf and flower designs can be found on Indian and Chinese objets d'art of the same period.

India and China have continued to influence embroidery and the table cover illustrated is typical of decoration of the Kashmiri region of India. This type of embroidery is worked either with a tambour hook or in chain stitch, on cream-colored even-weave fabric of close weave. Crewel yarn or spinning yarn is used for the embroidery, colors being limited to soft, subtle tones with one or two stronger hues to give gentle contrast to the design. The general effect of the embroidery is harmonious and flowing with no individual motif standing out from the others. In some examples of Indian-inspired embroidery, paillettes or pieces of mirror are used to add interest and additional contrast.

Daisy work 6

Design ideas in Teneriffe lace

Teneriffe lace is one of the few lacemaking techniques which can be worked from an illustration, without a pattern or working instructions. It is also something to experiment with by improvising and working out new design ideas. The textures of the yarns, the grouping of the spokes, the color combinations and additional decorative stitches combine to make innumerable design permutations.

Here are four examples of Teneriffe lace motifs to copy which may inspire further design ideas.

Apricot and yellow motif

All Teneriffe lace originates from the "sun" laces, and this particular motif has a very obvious sun-like center surrounded by a scroll effect. Based on a seventy-six spoke circle, there are thirty-eight open petals. A central row of knotting holds the spokes in twos. A second row of knotting runs parallel and the space between is darned in contrasting color. An outer ring of knotting in self color holds the petals in place, and halfway between the knotting and the darning a third color is used for interlacing to twist the spokes.

Yellow and blue open petal motif

There is a great feeling of movement in this motif—reminiscent of the optical illusory spin on the spokes of a turning wheel. Based on a seventy-six spoke circle, there are thirty-eight open petals. An outer row of knotting holds the spokes in twos, the next row repeats the same grouping and the third alternates. The space between the outer two circles is filled with darning, and Cretan stitch is worked between the middle and inner circles. An inner row of interlacing twists the spokes. All decoration is worked in the same contrasting color, the knotting in the main color.

Pink and green motif

This very symmetrical design is based on a circle of seventy-six spokes making thirty-eight open petals. The outer two rings of knotting group the threads in twos alternately, and between them is a ring of Cretan stitch. A further two rows of knotting groups the same threads and there is darning between these two rows. The inner row of interlacing is worked in contrasting color. All the knotting is worked in the main color, all decoration in contrasting.

Yellow and blue close petal motif

A more heavily worked motif, this is based on a circle of 138 spokes making sixty-nine petals. The central darning is worked in the contrasting color. Two rows of contrasting knotting group the threads in alternated twos. A third row of knotting in the main color groups the threads in sixes. Four of these are left free and two covered in contrasting color needleweaving alternately. Finally a row of interlacing in contrasting color twists the threads in groups of three.

▲ *Apricot and yellow motif*   ▼ *Yellow and blue open petal moti[f]*

▼ *Pink and green motif*   *Yellow and blue close petal motif* ▶

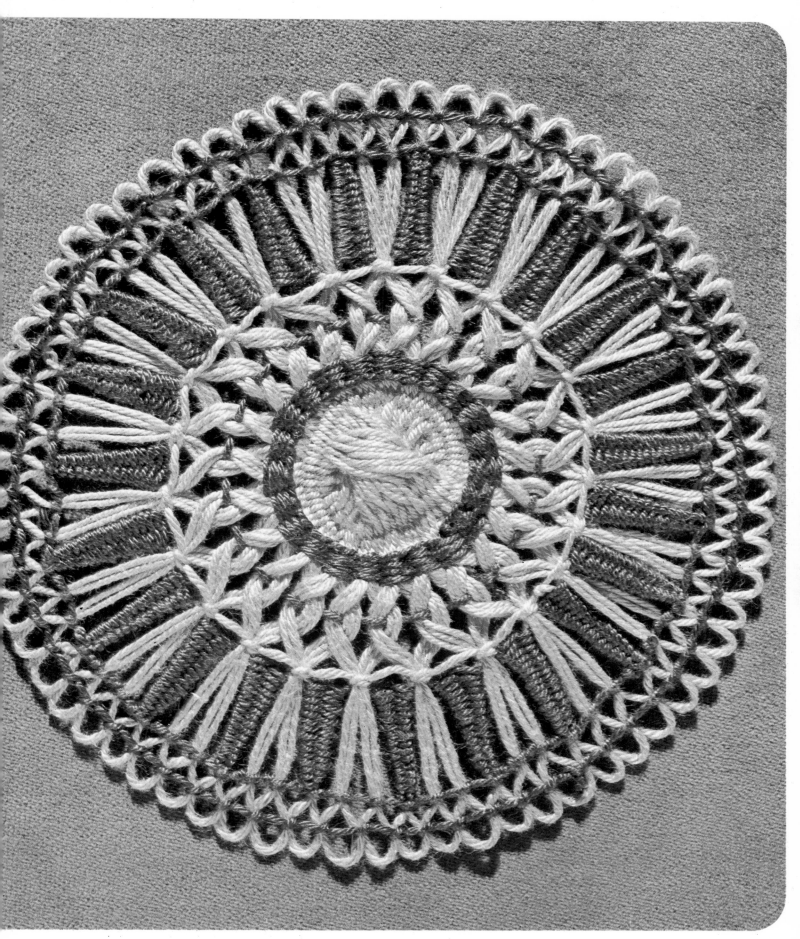

1195

Making hipster pants

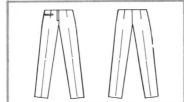

These hipster pants are a Pattern Pack adaptation. They are made in exactly the same way as the basic pants, except for the waist edge which is finished with a facing, and the addition of a bound pocket.

Suitable fabrics

Hipsters should be made in a firmly woven fabric which holds its shape well since they have to fit really close to the body.

Making the pattern

How low you wear the hipsters depends on the shape of your figure. The greater the difference between waist and hip measurement the more daring you can afford to be, but the pants will be most comfortable if they rest on the hipbone. These instructions are for the average figure shape and the pants are made to sit 3 inches below the waistline.

Use your favorite pants pattern, flared or straight, and find the position for the new waistline. Following the waistline curve on the pattern carefully, draw in the new waistline 3 inches below the original (figure **1**) and cut off the surplus.

To check that the new waist measurement is correct, measure yourself 3 inches below your natural waistline, add 1 inch to the measurement for ease and compare it to the new pattern waistline. Take any surplus into the darts and the side seams.

Taper each alteration line into the original line of the darts and seams at hip level. Do not alter the shape of the Center Front and the Center Back except for reasons of fitting.

You will also need facing patterns but these are left till the garment has been fitted and all adjustments made.

Make and fit the pants, except for the waist edge, as for the basic pants in Dressmaking chapters 36, page 716, and 37, page 734.

Making a bound pocket

This bound pocket is a simplified version of a tailored pocket and can be made very quickly. The pocket is set right through the dart and should be made before you finish the waist edge.

Mark the pocket position on one pant Front, $1\frac{1}{2}$ inches below the waistline, 3 inches from Center Front and $3\frac{1}{2}$ inches long (figure **2**).

Underlaying the pocket. First, underlay the pocket opening with a strip of soft interfacing $1\frac{1}{2}$ inches wide and $4\frac{1}{2}$ inches long, cut on the straight of grain.

Pin and baste the strip to the inside of the Front over the pocket position and mark the pocket position on the underlay (figure **3**).

Binding the pocket. The pocket binding and the front lining of the pocket are cut in one. For this you will need a piece of pants

fabric $5\frac{1}{2}$ inches wide by $6\frac{3}{4}$ inches long, cut on the crosswise grain of the fabric.

Mark the position of the pocket on the binding $1\frac{1}{2}$ inches from the upper edge, then pin the binding to the pants, right sides facing, as shown (figure **4**). Baste in place.

Working on the pocket underlay, make two rows of stitches the length of the opening and $\frac{1}{4}$ inch to each side of it (figure **5**).

Following figure **6**, cut the pocket opening between the stitching lines through all the layers of fabric as shown. Pull the binding through the opening and press the seam allowances away from the opening.

Roll the top of the binding down and the bottom up so that the binding meets at the center of the opening to form the bound edge (figure **7**). Baste in position as shown, then make small prick stitches along both seamlines, working from the front and stitching through all layers of fabric. Press and then remove the basting.

Lift the pocket lining so that you can get at the seam allowance at the lower edge of the pocket opening, then stitch the seam allowance to the pocket lining close to the seamline.

Carefully baste the bound edges of the pocket together on the right side (figure **8**), first pushing the unstitched ends under with the point of the needle to form a neat corner at each end.

Turn the work to the wrong side and stitch the loose triangular end at each side of the opening to the rolled edges (figure **9**).

Use a one-sided zipper foot so that you can work very close to the fold line at the sides of the pockets to secure the corners firmly.

Completing the pocket lining. The pocket back lining is taken into the waist seam for extra support, so cut a piece of pants fabric $5\frac{1}{2}$ inches wide by $7\frac{1}{4}$ inches long, on the straight grain of the fabric.

Pin it to the pocket front lining, to cover the bound edges and to reach the seam allowances at the waist edge (figure **10**).

Stitch the seam allowance of the upper bound edge to the binding and pocket back lining close to the seam.

Stitch the pocket linings together around the edges (figure **11**). On the outside of the pocket hand-work a small bar at each end of the opening to avoid strain on the corners of the pocket.

Making the facings for the waist edge

If you have made any alterations to the waistline during fitting, transfer these to the pattern.

Pin the darts on the pattern. Lay the upper section of the Center Front and Back to the straight edge of a sheet of paper and pin. Draw around the waist and side seam edges of the pattern to obtain the facings, then make them 2 inches deep as shown (figure **12**). Cut out the facings from double fabric, placing the Center Back on the fold and cutting the Center Fronts with seam allowance.

The waist edge also needs the support of an interfacing and stiff canvas is recommended for this. Cut out the interfacings as for the facings but without seam allowance along the lower edges. Overlap and stitch the side seams of the interfacing. Then, after the zipper is stitched in place, pin and baste the interfacing to the inside edge of the waistline of the pants.

Trim the Center Front edges of the interfacing so that they can be pushed under the seam allowance of the pants. Hand-sew the interfacing to the darts and seam allowances of the pants.

Stitch and press the side seams of the facing.

With right sides together, pin and baste the facing to the waist edge of the pants and stitch in position.

Trim the seam allowance, turn the facing to the inside, edge baste and press. Sew the facing to the zipper tape in the usual way.

For extra strength, and to stop the facing from rolling out during wear, topstitch the pants $\frac{1}{4}$ inch from the waist edge.

Finish lower facing edge and hand-sew lightly to seams and darts.

Fasten the opening at the top with a strong hook and eye (figure **13**).

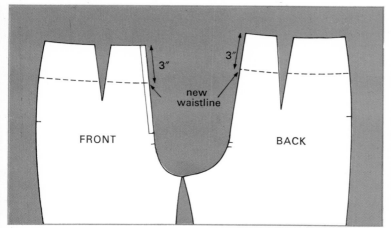

▲ **1.** *Finding the new waistline on the pattern*

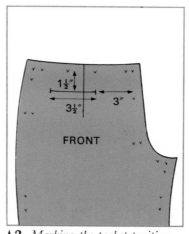

▲ **2.** *Marking the pocket position*

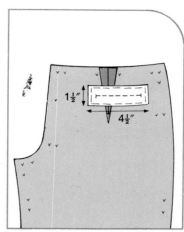

▲ **3.** *Positioning the underlay*

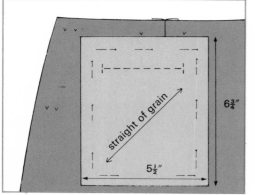

▲ **4.** *The binding pinned to the pocket opening*

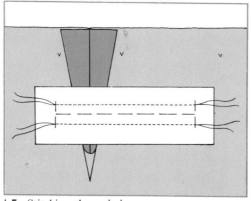

▲ **5.** *Stitching the underlay*

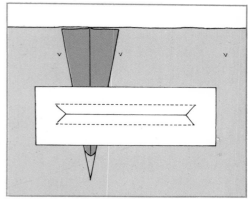

▲ **6.** *Cutting the pocket opening*

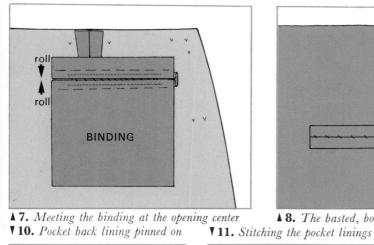

▲ **7.** *Meeting the binding at the opening center*

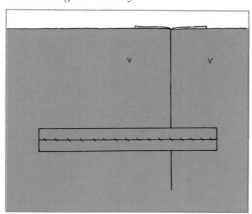

▲ **8.** *The basted, bound edges, corners neatened*

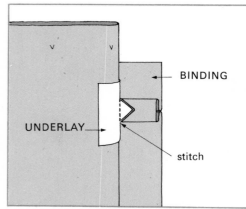

▲ **9.** *Securing the corners on the inside*

▼ **10.** *Pocket back lining pinned on* ▼ **11.** *Stitching the pocket linings* ▼ **12.** *Making the facings* ▼ **13.** *The finished front opening*

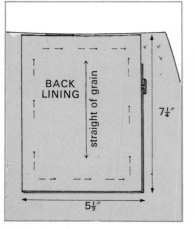

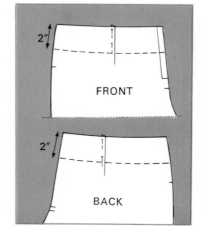

Three Aemilia-ars lace motifs

Add the three Aemilia-Ars motifs in this chapter to your repertoire. All of them include stitches and techniques from Needle-made lace chapter 5. With practice, it is possible to work straight from an illustration without guide lines. Begin designing your own motifs by interchanging parts of these, such as the corner of the star with the petal center, gradually introducing new ideas until a completely original motif evolves.

Making motifs without patterns

Once you have mastered the techniques of Aemilia-Ars lace, it is possible to make motifs by following illustrations.

If a basic skeleton of the design is not provided, make one from the illustration and then work the motif by following the basic steps given in Needle-made lace chapter 5.

Broadly speaking, the simplest method is to work the corners first with their diagonals, starting at the top left-hand corner, followed by the bottom left-hand corner, then the top right-hand corner. Next, work the center motifs from the middle outward and finish with the last remaining corner. It is usually possible, in this way, to avoid breaking the thread at any stage.

Each of the three motifs given in this chapter has a pretty, snowflake effect. The charts of the basic outlines are used actual size working with D.M.C. Pearl Cotton No.8 or they can be enlarged to use a thicker yarn. The designs are mostly worked in cording and buttonhole stitch enriched with picots. The spokes of the lace star motif are worked in spaced buttonhole stitch. The illustrations are enlarged to make the stitches clearer.

Once the motif is completed, remove it from the supporting bars and insert it in fabric using buttonhole stitch as illustrated. or sew several together.

▲ *The actual size tracing pattern for the lace star motif illustrated below left*

▲ *The tracing pattern for the wheel star motif which is illustrated below center*

▲ *The tracing pattern for the petal motif which is illustrated below right*

Collector's Piece

Cats in needlepoint

Louis J. Gartner, who designed and executed these realistic looking pieces of needlepoint, puts together his designs for needlepoint by "borrowing" the elements, sometimes from magazine and book illustrations.

The leopard cub was taken from a magazine illustration and enlarged to lifesize to fit into a circle fourteen inches in diameter. The original picture was full of small detail which made the designer decide to work the animal itself in petit point against a gros point background. To reproduce the plump roundness of a live animal and the subtlety of the baby fur, Louis J. Gartner used twelve different "fur" colored yarns plus black and white. The shaded background to the animal was achieved by working colors in slanting stripes so that the tones blended imperceptibly, giving an effect of space behind the cub. The tiger's head was "borrowed", just as it is, from a record album design. The designer began this piece by working the eyes and mouth first, feeling that if he got the expression right from the beginning, the animal would have an identity for the rest of the design. The interesting grass effect in the background was inspired by a piece of *strié* velvet; the velvet was subsequently used for the back of the cushion.

The reclining tiger, originally enlarged from a small magazine illustration, has been simplified into stylized lines with little detail or shading. The design has been worked in petit point using silk thread and the finished piece made into a pincushion, eight inches wide.

Louis J. Gartner Jr., is the author of *Needlepoint Design* published by William Morrow & Co. Inc.

Introduction to fisherman knitting

Try knitting a fisherman's traditional seamless pullover. Around the coast of England and Scotland, wherever there are fishing fleets and fishermen, there can still be found examples of the traditional seamless pullover correctly called guernsey. While the guernseys are basically alike, each area has an individual style—some have distinctive yokes, others have vertical panel designs and some have horizontal patterns. Apart from regional styles each village, and even individual families, have their own designs. Some even have the initials of the owner worked into the pattern.

The designs are never haphazard, but use symbols to tell a story reflecting the fisherman's surroundings, family life and the tools of his trade.

Seamless knitting

The guernsey is knitted circularly, cast on with a set of four or five double pointed needles at the lower edge and worked in one up to the beginning of the armholes. The work then divides and the back and front are worked separately to the shoulders, which are bound off together.

This binding off is often on the right side to give a decorative ridge. The neckband is then worked circularly again, although in Scotland buttons and buttonholes would be added at the shoulder.

To give greater ease of movement, a gusset is often made just before the armhole division and carried on into the top of the sleeves, which are then picked up and knitted down-

ward to the cuff. Although entirely seamless, a mock seam is often worked at either side. The gusset is increased in the center of the seam and the seam carried on down the sleeve once the gusset is completed.

Types of wool

The guernsey is not unlike a patterned brocade when finished and is always knitted on fine needles. The wool traditionally used is often as thick as knitting worsted or thicker, but it is made firm and weatherproof by the closeness of the stitches.

Anchor design

One of the many designs seen on guernseys on the coast of Fife in Scotland is the Anchor pattern, which can be worked as a repeat across the work or repeated upward in a vertical panel. It repeats over a number of stitches divisible by 21.

1st row. *P2, K1, P2, K11, P2, K1, P2, rep from * to end.
2nd row. *K2, P1, K2, P11, K2, P1, K2, rep from * to end. Rep 1st and 2nd rows once more.
5th row. *P2, K1, P2, K5, P1, K5, P2, K1, P2, rep from * to end.
6th row. *K2, P1, K2, P4, K1, P1, K1, P4, K2, P1, K2, rep from * to end.
7th row. *P2, K1, P2, K3, (P1, K1) twice, P1, K3, P2, K1, P2, rep from * to end.
8th row. *K2, P1, K2, P2, K1, P5, K1, P2, K2, P1, K2, rep from * to end.
9th row. *P2, K1, P2, K1, P1, (K3, P1) twice, (K1, P2) twice, rep from * to end.

10th row. *(K2, P1) twice, K1, P7, K1, (P1, K2) twice, rep from * to end.
11th row. *P2, K1, P2, K5, P1, K5, P2, K1, P2, rep from * to end.
12th row. As 2nd.
13th row. As 11th.
14th row. As 2nd.
15th row. *P2, K1, P2, K3, P5, K3, P2, K1, P2, rep from * to end.
16th row. *K2, P1, K2, P3, K5, P3, K2, P1, K2, rep from * to end.
17th row. As 15th.
18th row. As 2nd.
19th row. As 11th.
20th row. As 2nd.
21st row. As 11th.
22nd row. *K2, P1, K2, P4, K1, P1, K1, P4, K2, P1, K2, rep from * to end.
23rd row. *P2, K1, P2, K3, (P1, K3) twice, P2, K1, P2, rep from * to end.
24th row. As 22nd.
25th row. As 11th.
26th row. As 2nd.
Rep 1st-26th rows for patt.

Sheringham design

This pattern was taken from a patterned yoke edged with ridged purl welts and shows patterning at its best. The pattern repeats over a number of stitches divisible by 24.

K2 rows. P2 rows.
Rep last 4 rows 3 times more. Begin diamond pattern.
1st row. *K6, P1, K11, P1, K5, rep from * to end.
2nd row. *P4, K1, P1, K1, P9, K1, P1, K1, P5, rep from * to end.
3rd row. *K4, P1, K3, P1, K7, P1, (K1, P1) twice, K3, rep from * to end.
4th row. *P2, K1, (P1, K1) 3 times, (P5, K1) twice, P3, rep from * to end.
5th row. *K2, P1, K7, P1, K3, P1, (K1, P1) 4 times, K1, rep from * to end.
6th row. *K1, (P1, K1) 6 times, P9, K1, P1, rep from * to end.
7th row. *P1, K11, P12, rep from * to end.
8th row. *K11, P1, K1, P9, K1, P1, rep from * to end.
9th row. *K2, P1, K7, P1, K13, rep from * to end.
10th row. *P14, K1, P5, K1, P3,

rep from * to end.
11th row. *K4, P1, K3, P1, K15, rep from * to end.
12th row. *P16, K1, P1, K1, P5, rep from * to end.
Rep 1st—12th rows for patt.

Flag and cable design

This pattern is seen in designs from the Scottish and Yorkshire coastal areas, and can be used as an all over design or in narrow panels separated by seed stitch panels or cable panels.

Repeat the pattern over a number of stitches divisible by 26.

1st row (right side). *P2, K1, P2, slip next 3 sts onto cable needle and hold at back of work, K3, K3 from cable needle, P2, K1, P2, K2, P8, rep from * to end.
2nd row. *K7, P3, K5, P6, K5, rep from * to end.
3rd row. *P2, K1, P2, K6, P2, K1, P2, K4, P6, rep from * to end.
4th row. *K5, P5, K5, P6, K5 rep from * to end.
5th row. *P2, K1, P2, K6, P2, K1, P2, K6, P4, rep from * to end.
6th row. *K3, P7, K5, P6, K5, rep from * to end.
7th row. *P2, K1, P2, K6, P2, K1, P2, K8, P2, rep from * to end.
8th row. *K1, P9, K5, P6, K5, rep from * to end.
Rep 1st-8th rows for patt.

Pine tree design

This design is found in many variations, usually on guernseys belonging to Scottish fishermen. It can be used separately as a motif, or in conjunction with seed stitch borders and diamonds.

The pattern is worked over a number of stitches divisible by 15.

1st row. (right side). K.
2nd row. P.
3rd row. *K7, P1, K7, rep from * to end.
4th row. *P6, K1, P1, K1, P6, rep from * to end.
5th row. *K5, P1, K3, P1, K5, rep from * to end.
6th row. *P4, (K1, P2) twice, K1, P4, rep from * to end.
7th row. *K3, P1, K2, P1, K1,

P1, K2, P1, K3, rep from * to end.

8th row. *(P2, K1) twice, P3, (K1, P2) twice, rep from * to end.

9th row. *K1, (P1, K2) twice, P1, (K2, P1) twice, K1, rep from * to end.

10th row. *P3, K1, P2, K1, P1, K1, P2, K1, P3, rep from * to end.

11th row. *K2, P1, K2, P1, K3, P1, K2, P1, K2, rep from * to end.

12th row. *P4, K1, P2, K1, P2, K1, P4, rep from * to end.

13th row. *K3, P1, K2, P1, K1, P1, K2, P1, K3, rep from * to end.

14th row. *P5, K1, P3, K1, P5, rep from * to end.

15th row. *K4, P1, (K2, P1) twice, K4, rep from * to end.

16th row. *P6, K1, P1, K1, P6, rep from * to end.

17th row. *K5, P1, K3, P1, K5, rep from * to end.

18th row. *P7, K1, P7, rep from * to end.

19th row. *K6, P1, K1, P1, K6, rep from * to end.

20th row. P.

21st row. As 3rd.

22nd row. P.

Rep 1st-22nd rows for patt.

▼ *Anchor design*

▲ *Sheringham fishermen wearing their guernseys, two in similar patterns*

▼ *Pine tree design*

▲ *Sheringham design*   ▼ *Flag and cable design*

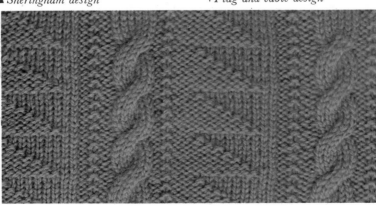

Lacy-sleeved for a little girl

Here is a pretty dress to crochet for a little girl's special occasions. It is worked in a soft, lightweight yarn in basic stitches.

Sizes

Directions are for 23in chest. The figures in brackets [] refer to the 24 and 25in sizes respectively.
Length at center back, 17¾[18½:19¼]in.
Sleeve seam, 8¾[9¼:9¾]in.

Gauge

18sc and 25 rows to 4in worked on No.E crochet hook

Materials

3-ply fingering yarn
7[7:9] ounces
One No. E (3.50 mm) crochet hook
One small button

Front

Using No.E crochet hook ch69[72:75].
1st row Into 2nd ch from hook work 1sc, 1sc into each ch to end. Turn.
2nd row Ch1, *1sc in next sc, rep from * to end. Turn.
Continue in sc, dec one sc at each end of 9th and every following 10th row 5 times in all. 59[62:65]sc.
Continue without shaping until work measures 12½[13:13½]in from beg.

Shape armholes

1st row Ss over 3sc, work in sc to last 3sc. Turn.
2nd row Work in sc to end. Turn.

3rd row Ss over 2sc, work in sc to last 2sc. Turn.
4th row Work in sc to end. Turn.
Rep 3rd and 4th rows once more.
Next row Ss over 1sc, work in sc to last sc. Turn. 43[46:49]sc.
Continue without shaping until armholes measure 2¾[3:3¼]in from beg.

Shape neck

Next row Ch1, 1sc into each of next 15[16:17]sc. Turn.
Complete left shoulder first.
Continue in sc, dec 2sc at beg of next row and 1sc at beg of every other row once.
Continue without shaping until armhole measures 4¾[5:5¼]in from beg, ending at armhole edge.

Shape shoulder

1st row Ss over 5sc, work in sc to end. Turn.
2nd row Work in sc to end. Turn.
3rd row Ss over 4sc, work in sc to end. Fasten off.
With RS of work facing, skip center 11[12:13]sc, attach yarn to last 16[17:18]sc and work right shoulder as for left shoulder, reversing shaping.

▼*Close-up of lace sleeve stitch*

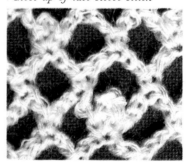

Back

Using No.E crochet hook ch62[66:70].
Work as given for Front, dec one st at each end of 11th and every following 12th row 4 times in all. 54[58:62]sc.
Continue without shaping until Back measures same as Front to underarm.

Shape armholes

1st row Ss over 2sc, work in sc to last 2sc. Turn.
2nd row Work in sc to end. Turn.
Rep 1st and 2nd rows once more.
5th row Ss over 1sc, work in sc to last sc. Turn. 44[48:52]sc.
Continue without shaping until armhole measures 1in from beg.

Divide for back opening

Next row Ch1, work 1sc into each of next 21[23:25]sc. Turn.
Complete right back first.
Continue working in sc until armhole measures same as Front to shoulder, ending at armhole edge.

Shape shoulder

1st row Ss over 5sc, work in sc to end. Turn.
2nd row Work in sc to end. Turn.
3rd row Ss over 4sc, work in sc to end. Fasten off.
With RS of work facing, attach yarn to rem sts and work left back as for right back, reversing shaping.

Sleeves

Using No.E crochet hook ch23[25:27].
1st row Into 2nd ch from hook work 1sc, 1sc into each ch to end. Turn.
2nd row Ch1, *1sc into next sc, rep from * to end. Turn.
3rd row Ch3, skip 1sc, 1sc into next sc, *ch2 skip 1sc, 1sc into next sc, rep from * to end. Turn. 11[12:13] sps.
4th row *Ch5, 1sc into next ch2 sp, rep from * to end. Turn.

5th row *Ch5, 1sc into 3rd ch of ch5 sp of previous row, rep from * to end. Turn.
6th row *Ch5, 1sc into next sp, ch3, 1sc into same sp as last sc—called 1 picot—ch5, 1sc into next sp, rep from * to last 1[0:1] sp, ch5, 1 picot in last sp[0:ch5, 1 picot in last sp]. Turn.
7th row As 5th.
8th row *Ch5, 1sc into next sp, ch5, 1 picot into next sp, rep from * to last 1[0:1] sp, ch5, 1sc in last sp[0:ch5, 1sc in last sp]. Turn.
Rows 5-8 form patt and are rep throughout.
Continue in patt until sleeve measures 8¾[9¼:9¾]in from beg, or desired length to underarm.

Shape cap

Next row Keeping patt correct, ss over ch2 to center of first ch sp, 1sc into 3rd ch of ch5 loop, work in patt to last sp, 1sc into 3rd of last ch5 loop. Turn.
Rep the last row 8 times more. Fasten off.

Sleeve frill

Using No.E crochet hook and with RS of sleeve facing, work frill along lower edge.
1st row Attach yarn to first sc, *ch5, 1sc into next sc, rep from * to end. Turn.
2nd row As 5th row of sleeve patt. Fasten off.

Collar

Using No.E crochet hook ch47[49:51].
1st row Into 2nd ch from hook work 1sc, 1sc into each ch to end. Turn.
Work 2 rows sc.
4th row As 3rd of sleeve patt.
5th row As 4th of sleeve patt.
6th row As 5th of sleeve patt. Fasten off.

Finishing

Press lightly.
Join shoulder, side and sleeve seams. Sew in sleeves. Sew collar around neck edge. Work a loop buttonhole at top of back opening. Sew on button to correspond.

1205

Elegant trims in crochet

Shaped, detachable collars and cuffs in decorative stitches make charming trims for simple dresses.

Cuffs and collar with jabot

Size
Cuff. Shortest edge about 6in
Collar. About 10½in around neck
Jabot. Depth about 6¼in

Materials
Coats & Clark's O.N.T. Pearl Cotton
3 balls
One No.B crochet hook
Three hooks and eyes

Cuffs
Ch46.
1st row Work 1sc into 2nd ch from hook, 1sc into each ch to end.
Work 1ss in end of ch, ch3, then work 44dc along other side of foundation ch. Turn.
2nd row Ch3, *skip 1 st, (yoh, insert hook into next st, yoh, draw loop through, yoh, draw yarn through 2 loops on hook), rep 3 times, yoh and draw through all loops—called 1cl—, ch5, skip 1 st, 1sc into next st, ch5, rep from * ending with 1cl, ch1, skip 1 st, 1dc into turning ch. Turn.
3rd row Ch2, *1sc into sp before cl, ch3, 1sc into sp after cl, ch5, rep from * ending with 1sc after last cl, 1dc into turning ch. Turn.
4th row Ch3, *cl into ch3 loop, ch6, 1sc into ch5 loop, ch6, rep from * ending with 1 cl, ch1, 1dc into turning ch. Turn.

1206

5th row Ch1, 1sc in sp before cl, *ch5, 1sc in sp after cl, ch5, 1sc into same loop, ch5, 1sc into next loop, ch5, 1sc into same loop before cl again, rep from * ending with ch5, 1sc after cl, 1sc into turning ch. Turn.
6th row Ch 1 * 2sc into next loop, work 1 picot of ch4 and join with ss into first ch, 2sc into same loop, rep from * into each loop of ch of the previous row, ending with ss into last sc. Fasten off. Sew on hook and eye.

Work second cuff in the same way.

Collar with jabot
Ch82. Turn.
Work 1 row following directions for cuff, working 81sc, 1ss, ch3 and 80dc. Leave this piece with yarn attached.
Using a 2nd ball of yarn, prepare center frill of jabot. Ch36, into 2nd ch from hook work 1sc, 1sc into each ch to end. 35sc. Into same st work 4sc to round end and 1sc to form first st of second side, then work 34sc along other side of foundation ch. Turn.
Ch3, work 34dc to corner, 2dc into each of 4 corner sc, 35dc along other side. Join to center of dc on collar piece with 5sc. Fasten off.
Return to yarn on collar piece, work all around the collar and center frill, except for the sc row on the collar, as given in the directions for the cuffs, on the 1st row working 1cl in first inc dc, 1cl between 2dc at end and 1cl in last inc dc.
Sew on hook and eye.

Picot stitch cuffs and collar

Size
Cuff. Wrist edge about 7in
Collar. Neck edge about 13in

Materials
Coats & Clark's O.N.T. Pearl Cotton
3 (50 yd.) balls
One No. B (2.00 mm.) crochet hook
Three hooks and eyes

Cuffs
Ch46 loosely.
1st row Into 2nd ch from hook work 1sc, 1sc into each ch to end. Turn.
2nd row Ch1, work 1sc into each sc. Turn.
3rd row Ch4, skip 1sc, *(yoh, insert hook into next st, yoh, draw loop through, yoh, draw yarn through 2 loops on hook) 3 times into same st, yoh, draw through all loops—called 1cl —, ch2, skip 1sc, 1sc into next sc, ch2, skip 1sc, rep from * ending with 1cl, ch2, 1dc into last sc. Turn. 11cl.
4th row Ch5, *2sc in top of cl, ch5, rep from * ending with ch3, 1dc into 2nd ch. Turn.
5th row Ch1, 3sc into ch3 loop picking up back loop of each st only, *1sc into each of 2sc over cl again picking up back loop only, skip ch1, 1sc into each of next 4ch of next loop picking up back loop only, rep from * ending 3sc. Turn.
6th row Ch1, 1sc into each sc picking up both loops. Turn. 68sc.
7th row Ch5, into 5th sc work *1cl, ch3, skip 2sc, 1sc into next sc, ch3, skip 2sc, rep from * ending with 1cl, ch2, skip 2sc, 1dc into last sc. Turn. 11cl.
8th row Ch5, *2sc in top of cl, ch6, rep from * ending with ch2, 1dc into 3rd of turning ch. Fasten off.
Beg at base of cuff, attach yarn and work along short edge as follows:

1st row Ch1, 1sc in end of first sc row, 1sc in end of 2nd sc row, 2sc into next sp, 1sc in next row end, 2sc into next sp, 1sc in each of next 2sc row ends, 2sc into next sp, 1sc in next row end, 2sc in sp formed by last dc of last row, 1sc into top of dc at corner, 2sc into next ch2 picking up back loop only, *1sc into each of next 2sc picking up back loop only, skip 1st ch, 1sc into each of next ch4 picking up back loop only, skip ch1, rep from * ending with 3sc in ch3, 2sc into same sp to start 2nd short side, 1sc in row end, 2sc into next sp, 1sc in each of next 2sc row ends, 2sc into next sp, 1sc in row end, 2sc into next sp, 1sc in each of next 2sc row ends. Turn.
2nd row Ch1, 1sc into each sc picking up both loops and working 2sc into 15th and 81st sc to form corners. Turn.
3rd row Ch3, into 4th sc work 1cl, *skip 2 sts, ch3, 1sc, ch3, skip 2 sts, 1cl, rep from * ending with ch3, 1sc. Turn. 16cl.
4th row Ch2, *1sc into top of cl, work 1 picot of ch5 and join with ss to first ch, 1sc into top of cl, ch2, 1 picot, ch2, rep from * ending with ch2, 1sc.
5th row Ch3, work 1 row of dc along opposite edge of foundation row. Fasten off. Sew on hook and eye.
Work second cuff in same manner.

Collar
Ch96 loosely.
1st row Into 2nd ch from hook work 1sc, 1sc into each ch to end. Turn.
2nd row As cuff.
3rd row As cuff. 24cl.
4th and 5th rows As cuff.
6th row As cuff.
7th row As cuff. 24cl.
8th row As cuff. Fasten off.
Work edging as for cuff.
1st row As cuff.
2nd row As cuff, inc for corners on 15th and 160th sc.
3rd row As cuff. 29cl.
4th and 5th rows As cuff. Fasten off. Sew on hook and eye.

Picot stitch cuff opened flat ▲   *Picot stitch collar and cuffs* ▼

Cluster stitch collar, jabot and cuffs ▲   *Cluster stitch cuff opened flat* ▼

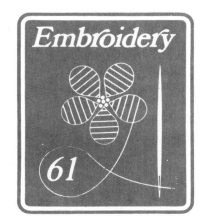

Hardanger tablecloth

To make a tablecloth measuring 34 inches square you will need:
- ☐ Cream colored Hardanger fabric—with 48 threads to 2 inches, 40in by 40in
- ☐ D.M.C. Pearl Cotton No.5, 7 skeins dark pink 893; 3 skeins light pink 894
- ☐ D.M.C. 6-cord crochet cotton No. 20, 1 ball 20gr snow-white
- ☐ Pink and cream sewing thread
- ☐ Tapestry needle No. 18

Planning the design

Use the counted thread guide to plan the outlines of the design. First trace a cross with basting thread following the grain of the fabric to find the center (shown in red on the counted thread guide). Working from the marked center, trace the outlines of the borders and squares in running stitches using matching thread. The figures on the guide represent the number of ground threads. The extreme outer line indicates the edge of the cloth after the hem has been turned. When planning the cloth, count another 30 threads all around for the hem.

To strengthen the borders

Strengthen the parts to be openworked by working a row of back-stitches inside the motifs with the pink sewing thread, six ground threads from the traced outline. Following the working charts A, B and C, embroider the triangular motifs in satin stitch using D.M.C. Pearl Cotton No. 5, so that the points of the triangles touch the traced outlines. Use chart C for the center border, chart B for outer center border, chart B for squares and chart A for the outer border. Each square on the charts represents one thread of the fabric. Each thick line represents one straight stitch. Use the light pink thread for the squares and the dark pink thread for the center and outer borders.

The openwork squares

To work the openwork squares, cut and draw 4 threads on all four sides, immediately below the pink satin stitch triangles. Then leave 8 threads, draw 8 and leave 8 alternately across and down the square. Work the cut openwork using D.M.C. 6-cord crochet cotton following the step-by-step diagrams. Work the inside border in the same way as for the square. For the openwork of the outside border, cut and draw 8 threads along each of the four sides of the tablecloth. Tie groups of 8 threads together with a blanket stitch. In the corners make a cross of threads and tie the center of the cross with a blanket stitch. Continue the border in the same way on the remaining three sides of the cloth.

Finishing

When all the embroidery has been completed, make a handkerchief hem on the cloth, following the instructions given in Embroidery chapter 21, page 414. Press on the wrong side.

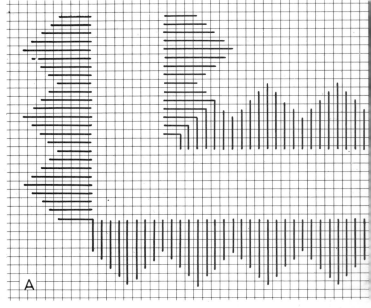

▲ Chart A for both edges of openwork border on tablecloth hem

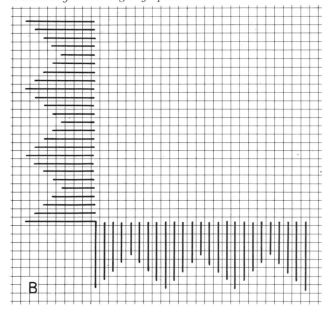

▲ Chart B for outer edge of central openwork and edges of squares

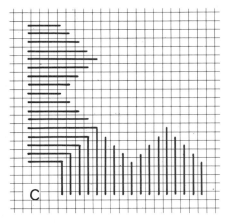

▲ Chart C for working the inner edge of central openwork

▲ *The openwork squares are edged in light pink, the central and hem areas edged in dark pink*

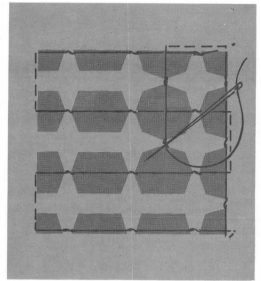

▲ *Openwork stages one and two*

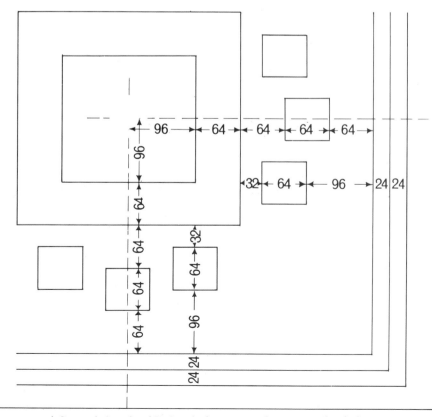

▲ *Counted thread guide for placing openwork areas on the cloth*

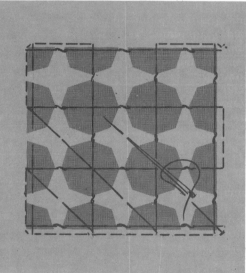

▲ *Openwork stage three*

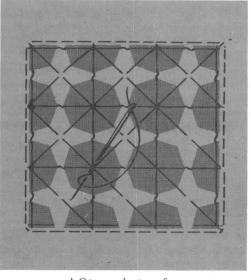

▲ *Openwork stage four*

Pattern Library

Golden Rose

Simple designs such as this full-blown rose can be used as a single motif, enlarged for a pillow or reduced small enough to make an all-over pattern on an evening bag, by working on coarse or fine mesh canvas, over more or fewer threads. For instance, using canvas with 10 double threads to the inch and working over two sets of double threads each way, the motif would measure $3\frac{3}{4}$ inches square. The colors used for the sample illustrated in D.M.C. Tapestry yarns are: red 7136, orange 7947, yellow 7435, green 7346, pastel green 7772, pale green 7771, dark blue 7306, terra cotta 7459. Or work to the colors of your favorite rose.